THE MYSTERY OF THE ALBANY MUMMIES

THE MYSTERY OF THE ALBANY MUMMIES

Edited by Peter Lacovara and Sue H. D'Auria

excelsior editions

AN IMPRINT OF STATE UNIVERSITY OF NEW YORK PRESS

www.sunypress.edu

Cover image: Mummy board of Ankhefenmut. Third Intermediate Period, 21st Dynasty, ca. 1069–945 BC. Wood and pigment. Bab el-Gasus. British Museum, London, donated by the Government of the British Protectorate of Egypt, EA24797. Photograph courtesy of the Trustees of the British Museum.

Frontispiece: Coffin lid of Ankhefenmut. Third Intermediate Period, 21st Dynasty, ca. 1069–945 BC. Wood and pigment. Bab el-Gasus. Kunsthistoriches Museum, Vienna, AE INV 6267a.

Published by
State University of New York Press, Albany

Excelsior Editions is an imprint of State University of New York Press

For information, contact
State University of New York Press, Albany, NY
www.sunypress.edu

Book design: click! Publishing Services
Production: Jenn Bennett-Genthner
Marketing: Kate Dias

Library of Congress Cataloging-in-Publication Data
Names: Lacovara, Peter, editor. | D'Auria, Sue, editor.
Title: The mystery of the Albany mummies / edited by Peter Lacovara and Sue D'Auria.
Description: Albany : Excelsior Editions/State University of New York Press, 2018. | Includes bibliographical references and index.
Identifiers: LCCN 2017027464 (print) | LCCN 2017028535 (ebook) | ISBN 9781438469508 (e-book) | ISBN 9781438469485 (paperback : alkaline paper)
Subjects: LCSH: Mummies—Egypt—History. | Mummy cases—Egypt—History. | Mummies—New York (State)—Albany—History. | Mummy cases—New York (State)—Albany—History. | Egyptology—New York (State)—Albany—History. | Albany Institute of History and Art—History. | Exhibitions—New York (State)—Albany—History. | Egypt—Kings and rulers—History. | Egypt—Antiquities.
Classification: LCC DT62.M7 (ebook) | LCC DT62.M7 M94 2018 (print) | DDC 932/.015—dc23
LC record available at https://lccn.loc.gov/2017027464

10 9 8 7 6 5 4 3 2 1

CONTENTS

All ancient dates are approximate.

Roman Period	30 BC–AD 395
Byzantine Period	395–642

EGYPT IN THE MIDDLE AGES

Muslim conquest of Egypt	639
Rashidun caliphate	632–661
Umayyad Egypt	661–750
Abbasid Egypt	750–969
Fatimid Egypt	969–1171
Ayyubid Egypt	1171–1250
Mamluk Egypt	1250–1517

OTTOMAN EGYPT

Ottoman empire	1517–1867
French occupation of Egypt	1798–1801
Khedivate of Egypt	1867–1882

MODERN EGYPT

British occupation of Egypt	1882–1953
Sultanate of Egypt	1922–1953
Arab Republic of Egypt	1953–present

This book recounts a fascinating tale of the mystery of the Albany Mummies from their early acquisition in 1909 to their beloved status as Albany's Egyptian priest and priestess in the mid-twentieth century to the present, when their mystery was solved through the intersection of historical scholarship and science and technology. Key to this story was the planning and installation of a major exhibition called "GE Presents: The Mystery of the Albany Mummies," organized by the Albany Institute of History & Art (AIHA) and on view from September 21, 2013, until June 6, 2014.

The planning for this exhibition and book began over nine years ago, when guest exhibition curator Dr. Peter Lacovara (who at that time served as senior curator of ancient Egyptian, Nubian, and Near Eastern art at the Michael C. Carlos Museum at Emory University in Atlanta, Georgia) confirmed that the mummy board for our Twenty-First Dynasty coffin belonging to Ankhefenmut, a sculptor and priest at the Temple of Mut, was in the collections of the British Museum, and Ankhefenmut's coffin lid was in the Kunsthistorisches Museum in Vienna. It was Lacovara's idea to mount a major exhibition to reunite the coffin parts for the first time in over 100 years and obtain new X-rays and CT scans of our mummies, which led to the resexing of the 21st Dynasty mummy and the confirmation that this was none other than the priest Ankhefenmut, rather than an unknown priestess, as previously thought.

The exhibition featured more than 350 objects with 140 major loans from the British Museum, London; Brooklyn Museum; Kunsthistorisches Museum, Vienna; Phoebe A. Hearst Museum of Anthropology, University of California, Berkeley; Semitic Museum, Harvard University; American Museum of Natural History, New York; Metropolitan Museum of Art, New York; Museum of Fine Arts, Boston; Michael C. Carlos Museum, Emory University; University of Pennsylvania Museum of Anthropology and Archaeology; Williams College Museum of Art; Albany Masonic Hall Association; Olana State Historic Site: NYS Office of Parks, Recreation and Historic Preservation; and Redwood Library and Athenaeum, Newport, Rhode Island. Private lenders included the Allen Anawati family; Susan Bachelder; Samuel and Lillian Borofsky; Dr. Bob Brier and Pat Remler; Douglas L. Cohn, DVM; Dubroff Family Foundation; Dr. Jerome Eisenberg, Royal Athena Gallery; Dr. Marjorie M. Fisher; Dr. Joel A. Freeman; Richard and Joanne Gascoyne; Joseph A. Lewis; Yvonne Markowitz; Tom Noonan; Dr. Salima Ikram; Julia Schottlander; Tom Swope; and Nancy Roberts.

The exhibition was divided into four major themes.

- *From the Nile to the Hudson* recounted the story of the Albany Institute's acquisition of the two mummies and coffins from the Cairo Museum in 1909 by Samuel W. Brown. This section included the discovery of the priest's cache at Deir el-Bahri, the purchase of the mummies and coffins, and their dispersal throughout the world.
- *Egyptomania in the Empire State* highlighted early archaeological discoveries in Egypt and the revival of ancient Egyptian art and design. This section helped set the stage for the Albany Institute's acquisition of the mummies.
- *Ankhefenmut and His World* showcased the beautifully decorated coffin of Ankhefenmut, reunited in the

exhibition with its lid and mummy board. This section focused on Ankhefenmut's life as a priest in the Temple of Mut and his profession as a sculptor. Noninvasive CT scans and X-rays revealed new information about this mummy's age, profession, and sex.

- *Preparing for the Afterlife* explored mummification practices and the ritual preparation and burial practices in Egypt over thousands of years. This section featured the museum's Ptolemaic Period (305–330 BC) mummy, new X-ray and CT scan images, and a selection of animal mummies and funerary objects.

To complement the exhibition, Erika Sanger, director of education, organized a lecture series that brought the following scholars from around the world to Albany to highlight relevant scholarship related to Egyptology and the Albany Mummies: Dr. Peter Lacovara, Michael C. Carlos Museum, "The Mystery of the Albany Mummies"; Dr. Nicholas Reeves, Metropolitan Museum of Art, "Amenhotep's Mask and His Book of the Dead"; Anna Tobin D'Ambrosio, director, Munson-Williams-Proctor Museum of Art, "Shadow of the Sphinx: Ancient Egypt and Its Influence"; Joyce Haynes, independent scholar, "Reading Hieroglyphs"; Dr. Bob Brier, Long Island University, "Ankhefenmut from Temple to Museum"; Dr. Lanny Bell, professor emeritus, Brown University, "Pyramids, Mummies, and Magic"; Dr. Melinda Hartwig, Georgia State University, "Artistic Conventions in Ancient Egypt"; Dr. John Taylor, the British Museum, "Ancient Egyptian Coffins as Text"; Dr. Kara Cooney, UCLA, Musical Coffins: "Reuse in the 21st Dynasty"; Dr. Salima Ikram, American University in Cairo, "Mummifying Animals in Ancient Egypt"; and Dr. Violaine Chauvet, University of Liverpool, "Tanis and Karnak: Temples in the 21st Dynasty."

A film, *The Albany Mummies: Unraveling an Ancient Mystery* (written, directed, and produced by professors Mary Valentis and William Rainbolt of the University at Albany) accompanied the exhibition and was shown on the PBS station WMHT. The film, produced by Fardin Sanai, executive director of the University at Albany Foundation, was a collaborative effort among the Albany Institute of History & Art, Albany Medical Center, University at Albany Foundation, and the University at Albany College of Arts and Sciences and Center for Humanities, Arts, and TechnoSciences. Other credits include John Valentis as narrator; Steve Nealey as cinematographer; John Lyden as film editor; David Bourgeois for sound design; original music by White Lake Music & Post.

I extend our heartfelt thanks to Peter Lacovara for his vision, expertise, and effort in helping solve the mystery of the Albany Mummies. His persistence and belief that the 21st Dynasty mummy was male and therefore the priest Ankhefenmut became the focal point of the study. Key to solving this challenge was Bob Brier, senior research fellow at the Long Island University C.W. Post Campus, also known as "Mr. Mummy." Brier is an internationally known Egyptologist recognized for using noninvasive CT scans and X-rays to study ancient Egyptian mummies. He was ably assisted by a team at Albany Medical Center, including Dr. Phuong Vinh, radiologist; Dr. Michael Schuster, radiologist; Howard Mayforth, technologist; and Emily Johnson Chapin, technologist.

Lacovara assembled a distinguished team of scholars, specialists, and conservators to work on this project, each of whom contributed essays in this book. Special thanks to Joyce Haynes, Egyptologist and retired curator, Museum of Fine Arts, Boston, who worked with museum staff over the years to translate the hieroglyphs on Ankhefenmut's coffin and research his family genealogy, which is included in the essay "Ankhefenmut and His World," co-written by Lacovara and Haynes. Lacovara also wrote the essays "Albany's Ptolemaic Mummy and Late Period Funerary Arts" and "Egyptomania and the Empire State." Brier has generously lent his expertise to the museum on a variety of subjects related to ancient Egypt. His two essays for this book, "The Mummy of Ankhefenmut: A Scientific Investigation" and "The Ptolemaic

Mummy: A Scientific Investigation," recount the results of the X-rays and CT scans. Three essays add to the story of the museum's collections. The first one, by Andrew Oliver, highlights a collection of rare Egyptological volumes in the museum's collection. The second, "Egyptian Textiles in the Albany Institute," prepared by Peter Lacovara with help from textile conservator Patricia Ewer and textile specialists Karen Nicolson and Kathleen Munn, focuses on two of the remarkable textiles recently found under the mummy of Ankhefenmut. The third, by Leslie Gat and Erin Toomey, discusses the conservation of Ankhefenmut's coffin. Special thanks to Allison Munsell Napierski, AIHA digitization operation manager, for photographing and preparing most of the images for this book, including the list of AIHA collections. Tom Nelson, exhibition and graphic designer, prepared the diagrams for the translation of the hieroglyphs on Ankhefenmut's coffin and created the reconstruction drawing and painting of the priest's robe.

A variety of scholars, volunteers, and interns assisted the museum on this project, including Jason Applegate, Sue Ding, Dr. Edward Bleiberg, Alexandra Brisbin, Dr. Jonathan Elias, Kevin Franklin, Tom Hardwick, Dr. Regina Hölzl,

Dr. Richard Jasnow, Ellen Leerburger, Jessica Lux, Linda Mclean, Adriana Morales, Marcia Moss, Sophie Moss, Steve Ricci, Norman Rice, Daniel Russo, Patricia Search, Pascale Stain, Jodi Stevens, Amanda Stickney, Brynna Tussey, David Taylor, Dr. John Taylor, John Vasquez, Ben Watkins, and Daniel M. Warne.

Many thanks to the following AIHA staff members who worked on this project: Dr. W. Douglas McCombs, Kelsey Hyde, Sarah Clowe, Barbara Collins, Elizabeth Reiss, Nicole Peterson, Kate Pauly, Briana Thomas, Aine Leader-Nagy, Susan Hsu, Elizabeth Bechand, Joseph Benassi, and Janine Moon.

Special thanks to the J.M. Kaplan Fund/Furthermore grants for providing funds toward the publication of this book, and to Sue D'Auria for editing the manuscript.

In closing, I extend my heartfelt thanks to George R. Hearst III for his vision and enthusiastic support of this project, and the AIHA board of trustees for their ongoing support of new scholarship and museum programming.

Tammis Groft
Executive Director

ACKNOWLEDGMENTS
FOR FUNDERS

The Albany Institute of History & Art wishes to thank the following funders for their support:

GRANTS, FOUNDATION, AND CORPORATE

Institute of Museum and Library Services; GE; Standish Family Fund; Bender Family Foundation; Bank of America Charitable Foundation; Albany Food and Wine Festival; Sidney and Beatrice Albert Foundation; Albany County Convention and Visitors Bureau; Albany Medical Center; J.M. Kaplan Fund/Furthermore; New York Council for the Humanities; Woodland Hill Montessori School; Northeastern Association of the Blind at Albany; New York State United Teachers; UHY Advisors; Tabner, Ryan and Keniry.; International Center of the Capital Region; Archaeological Institute of America; A Better Bite; WMHT; and the *Times Union*.

BENEFACTORS

Mr. and Mrs. George R. Hearst III and Dr. Heinrich Medicus

PATRONS

Mr. and Mrs. Paul V. Bruno
Neil and Jane Golub
Mrs. Munir Jabbur
Mr. and Mrs. E. Stewart Jones, Jr.
Richard Keresy

Mr. Charles M. Liddle III
Mr. and Mrs. Peter J. Maloy
Courtney L. and Victor A. Oberting III
Ms. Patricia Perrella
Mr. and Mrs. J. Spencer Standish

SUSTAINERS

Mr. and Mrs. Thomas J. Baldwin Jr.
Dr. and Mrs. John Balint, M.D.
Mr. Robert W. Becker
Mr. and Mrs. Sheridan C. Biggs
Donald and Ann Eberle
Mr. and Mrs. Christopher Falvey
Mr. and Mrs. Peter G. Ten Eyck II
Dr. and Mrs. Richard L. Jacobs
Mr. Jay H. Jakovic Esq.

Ms. Sheila K. Lobel and Mr. Ira Lobel
Mr. and Mrs. Gus J. Mininberg
Richard and Karen Nicholson
Ms. Anne Putnam and Mr. Bill Shannon
Mrs. Richard F. Sonneborn
Ms. Christine L. Standish and Mr. Christopher H. Wilk
Mr. and Mrs. Darryl W. Teal
Mr. and Mrs. Louis R. Tomson

SPONSORS

Mr. John T. Allison

Ms. Anne Christman

Ms. Rae Clark

Drs. Paul J. and Faith B. Davis

Mrs. Elizabeth D. Doviak

Dr. and Mrs. Myron Gordon

Dr. and Mrs. Vittorio Fiorenza

Mr. and Mrs. Edward M. Jennings

Mrs. Jocelyn R. Jerry

Mr. and Mrs. Alden B. Kaplan

Dr. Martha L. Lepow

Stephen and Nancy Linehan

Ms. Sarah M. Pellman

Ms. Rosemarie V. Rosen

Mrs. Abbott Weinstein

Bonny Bouck Wilson

SUPPORTERS

Dr. and Mrs. John W. Abbuhl

Mr. and Mrs. Theodore S. Adams

Ms. Gloria M. Ballien

Ms. Nadine Baumgarten

Ms. Diane L. Bartholdi

Mr. and Mrs. John Belton

Mr. and Mrs. Ed Blanchard

C. Robie Booth and Helen Fitzgerald

Mr. Stewart C. Boschwitz

Ms. Mary Ellen Browarski

Ms. Lynne Bunnell

Mr. James J. Campbell

Miss Alice C. Cantwell

Frieda and Prentiss Carnell

Sally Carter

Ms. Judith J. Clough

Mr. Findlay Cockrell and Mrs. Marcia W. Cockrell

Mr. Richard S. Conti and Mr. Steven Snow

Krysia and Carl Cording

Mr. and Mrs. Roy J. Cornell

Donna M Crisafulli and Richard Kuhnmunch

Mrs. Elsa G. deBeer

Mrs. Kimmey C. Decker

Mr. and Mrs. Dis Maly, Jr.

Ms. Marijo Dougherty and Mr. Norman Bauman

Ms. Joan T. Doran

Mr. and Mrs. Herbert S. Ellis

Mr. and Mrs. Joseph Erkes

Jean Dugan and Ben Ford

Mr. and Mrs. Karl Felsen

Ms. Cynthia Fox and Mr. Russell Youngman

Janet E. Gargiulo

Mr. and Mrs. Lewis C. Gershman

Ms. Margaret-Mary Girzone

James and Cheryl Gold

David and Felice Gordis

Mr. and Mrs. John Hawn

Mrs. Virginia E. Henry

Mr. William Hetzer

John Hinchen

Ms. Kathy Hodges

Mrs. Helen P. Howe

Mary Elizabeth Jones

Marilyn and Stan Kaltenborn

Mr. and Mrs. Daniel G. Keenan

Gail Kendall and David Galletly

Ms. E. Helen Gardner

Mr. and Mrs. Harry Griffin

Dr. Harold N. Langlitz

Mrs. Ethel A. Lansing

Miss Christina M. Larsen

Betsy Lopez-Abrams and Andrew Viglucci

Ms. Marietta Lynch

Chuck and Barbara Manning

Jacqueline and Ralph Marino

Mr. Peter Meixner and Mrs. Donna Meixner

Lois and David McDonald

Patricia Mion

Mr. Kenneth P. Mortensen, Jr.

Mr. and Mrs. Stephen H. Muller

Ms. Jennifer Murphy and Mr. Paul Wehren

Margaret and Richard Nells

Mr. and Mrs. John H. Nickles

Mr. and Mrs. Daniel Nolan

Mrs. Dorothea O'Brien

Paul J. O'Brien

Ms. Carolyn Olsen and Mr. David Ellison

Mr. Thomas Pfeiffer

Mr. and Mrs. William B. Picotte

John Pipkin and Nancy Denton

Diana and Paul Praus

Scott Reul and Terri Thompson

Ms. Polly N. Rutnik

Susan M. Schmader

Ms. Geri Stewart and Mr. Frank F. Putallaz

Phil and Bunny Savino

Marie and Lawrence Shore

Mr. and Mrs. William M. Schaefer

Ms. Fumiko Shido

Mr. Frank F. Shipp

Caryl Silber

Ms. E. R. Silverberg

Mrs. Hazel P. Smith

Mr. and Mrs. Donald H. Sommers

Ms. Sandra Sorell

Ms. Barbara Stenson

Alex Streznewski and Bob Reilly

Susan and Bruce Stuart

Ms. Judith C. Tate

Mrs. Susan C. Thompson

Ms. Marian E. Tremblay

Deborah Lee Trupin

Dr. and Mrs. John E. Tucker

Mr. Harry E. Van Tuyl, Jr.

John Vadney

Ms. Susan Weber and Mr. Mark Bertozzi

Ms. Lois J. Wilson

Priscilla and Paul Wing

Michael P. Zavisky and Barbara Zavisky

Mr. Donald G. Zeilman

From the Nile to the Hudson
The Albany Mummies

Tammis K. Groft

The story of the Albany Mummies centers on two ancient Egyptian mummies and their coffins, one dating from the 21st Dynasty and the other from the Ptolemaic Period. In 1909, these mummies and coffin bases were acquired by Albany businessman Samuel W. Brown (1857–1940) from the Egyptian Museum, Cairo, for the Albany Institute and Historical and Art Society, the present-day Albany Institute of History & Art (AIHA). The story of their discovery in the priest's cache at Deir el-Bahri, purchase by Brown, transport by steamship from Cairo to New York City, and steamboat travel to Albany was covered extensively by the Albany newspapers. Since their arrival at the institute, the mummies have been on continuous exhibition and are the most popular, celebrated, and best remembered of the museum's collections. Visitors from grandparents to school-aged children can recount stories about their first encounter with the Albany Mummies and through them, ancient Egyptian history.

How did these ancient Egyptian mummies wind up at the Albany Institute? Their arrival is part of the evolution of the institute itself, which traces its origins to 1791 and the formation of the Society for the Promotion of Arts, Agriculture and Manufactures, which had the purpose of improving the state's economy and ensuring citizen welfare through advances in agricultural methods. In 1804, the group was reincorporated as the Society for the Promotion of Useful Arts (1804–1823). In 1823, the museum changed its name again to the Albany Lyceum of Natural History (1823–1824) and turned its attention to matters related to the flora and fauna of the region and elsewhere. In subsequent years, the organization changed its name several more times, but maintained similar objectives. The celebration of Albany's city charter bicentenary in 1886, which gathered more than 4,000 historic relics and works of art from the city's past and its leading families, initiated a change of course for the organization that steered it away from natural history.

By the early twentieth century, the organization conducted its first campaign to build its current building at 125 Washington Avenue. With its opening in 1907, President of the Board of Directors James Ten Eyck (1840–1910) described the museum as being just like the Metropolitan Museum of Art, the Brooklyn Museum, and the Philadelphia Museum of Art. Its collections became more diverse and included art, decorative arts, and historical and ethnographic artifacts from all over the world. The 1909 acquisition of two mummies from ancient Egypt was in keeping with that mission. In 1926, the museum changed its mission to concentrate on its regional heritage and refined its collecting policy to include art, decorative arts, historical objects, and manuscript materials with a documented relationship to the upper Hudson Valley from the seventeenth century to the present. The majority of European arts and ethnographic collections were deaccessioned, but the Albany Mummies remained and are today interpreted as part of the museum's history (figure 1).

FROM THE NILE TO THE HUDSON

Throughout the nineteenth and twentieth centuries, tourists from New York's Hudson Valley traveled to Egypt and returned with collections of antiquities, souvenirs, books, and photographs. The earliest documented record of the two Egyptian mummies in Albany dates to January 1, 1831. A popular establishment founded in 1808 called the Albany Museum, located on the corner of State Street and Market Street (now Broadway), placed the following advertisement in the 1831 Albany City Directory: "One Hundred and Fifty Thousand Curiosities, among which are two Egyptian Mummies, is open for inspection, everyday, accept [sic] Sunday. Admittance, 25ct."[1] By 1841, the Albany Museum was primarily used as a theater; eventually the curiosities were sold

to well-known Albany circus owner Dr. Gilbert A. Spaulding, who displayed them on one of his famous "Floating Palace" steamboats that plied the Mississippi River.

A late nineteenth-century collector of Egyptian antiquities, Armand de Potter (1850–1905), operated the European and World Tours travel agency in Albany from 1879 to 1899. He also edited and published an annual journal called *The Old World and European Guide*, which offered testimonials about his trips and traveling tips ranging from appropriate clothing to currency exchange rates. In 1893, de Potter opened a second office in New York City, where he eventually moved.

De Potter had been born in France and immigrated to the United States in 1878. After his marriage in 1879 to Annie Beckwith of Red Hook, New York, the couple moved to

Albany. De Potter was well educated and fluent in German, French, and English, which allowed him to obtain a teaching position at the Albany Female Academy (now the Albany Academy for Girls). As their professor of modern languages and literature, de Potter met many of Albany's elite, who may have joined his tours. In 1880, he received an honorary master's degree from Union College in Schenectady, and his wife began teaching French at the Albany Female Academy.

In 1882, de Potter resigned his position at the academy to devote all of his energies to his tourist agency. In the course of his travels, he assembled a large collection of Egyptian antiquities, including 270 pieces that he exhibited at the 1893 World's Columbian Exposition, which was accompanied by a catalog he prepared.[2] After the close of the exposition, de Potter lent his collection to the University of Pennsylvania; eventually the Brooklyn Museum purchased it in 1908 from his widow.[3]

It is possible that Albany mayor John Boyd Thacher (1847–1909) or members of the Lyon family, owners of a well-known Albany printing company, traveled to Egypt on one of de Potter's Land of the Pharaohs tours, which included stops at Cairo, Giza, Memphis, Saqqara, and Thebes (including Karnak and Luxor). Thacher wrote a letter in 1889 to Albany artist Will H. Low (figure 4), recounting his thoughts on an Egyptian mummy and the Historical Society (AIHA):

I can buy a mummy of a young lady still in the box in which they placed her two or three thousand little years ago, with the sandals still on her feet and in the wooden sarcophagus the very garlands her friends threw in as they passed about it, the flowers faded . . . . I would buy it, only I learn our Historical Society is apparently no more lively than the young lady.[4]

The Lyon family of Albany visited Egypt twice (figures 2 and 3), once around 1907 and again twenty-five years later.

PLEASE SHOW US A MUMMY

Given Albany's familiarity with ancient Egyptian culture through the display of mummies downtown from 1831 to 1841, de Potter's World Tours, and the popularity of ancient Egyptian mummies in general, it is not surprising that the Albany Institute was keen to acquire its own mummies for its new building on Washington Avenue. It is not known exactly when James Ten Eyck, president of the board of trustees, Cuyler Reynolds (1866–1934), who served as museum director from 1899 to 1909, and their good friend Samuel Winfield Brown developed the plan to acquire mummies for the museum. Ten Eyck and Brown worked for Bacon and Stickney, a purveyor of spices, teas, and coffees in Albany (Ten Eyck was associated with the company from 1865 until 1909, and Brown worked there from 1877 until 1940). Brown, a world traveler, crossed the Atlantic more than twenty times, including two trips (1905 and 1909) to Cairo with his wife, Rosa. During his 1909 visit, he purchased two Egyptian mummies and coffin bases

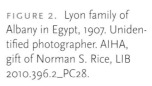

FIGURE 2. Lyon family of Albany in Egypt, 1907. Unidentified photographer. AIHA, gift of Norman S. Rice, LIB 2010.396.2_PC28.

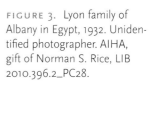

FIGURE 3. Lyon family of Albany in Egypt, 1932. Unidentified photographer. AIHA, gift of Norman S. Rice, LIB 2010.396.2_PC28.

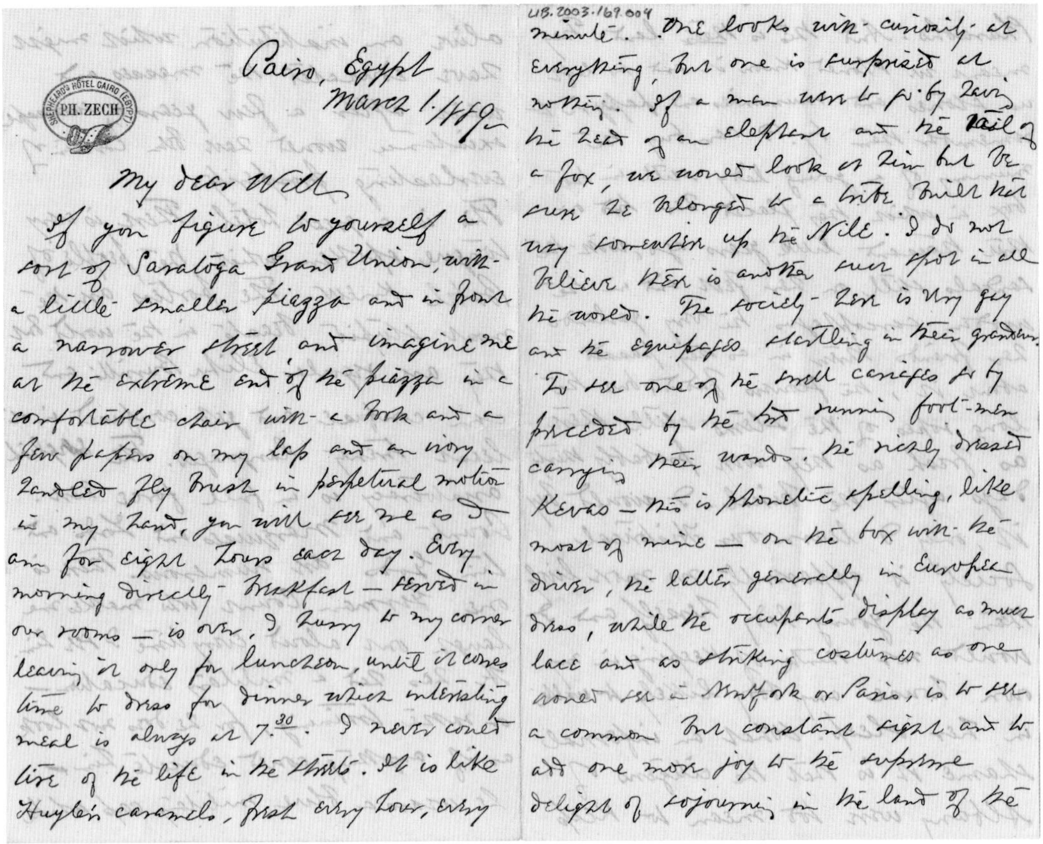

LIB.2003.169.004

SHEPHEARD'S HOTEL CAIRO (EGYPT)
PH. ZECH

Cairo, Egypt
March 1. 1889

My dear Will

If you figure to yourself a sort of Saratoga Grand Union, with a little smaller piazza and in front a narrower street, and imagine me at the extreme end of the piazza in a comfortable chair with a book and a few papers on my lap and an ivory handled fly brush in perpetual motion in my hand, you will see me as I am for eight hours each day. Every morning directly breakfast — served in our rooms — is over, I hurry to my corner leaving it only for luncheon, until it comes time to dress for dinner which interesting meal is always at 7.30. I never cease tire of the life in the streets. It is like Huyler's caramels, fresh every hour, every minute. One looks with curiosity at everything, but one is surprised at nothing. If a man were to go by having the head of an elephant and the tail of a fox, we would look at him but be sure he belonged to a tribe built here way somewhere up the Nile. I do not believe there is another such spot in all the world. The society here is very gay and the equipages startling in their grandeur. To see one of the small carriages go by preceded by the two running foot-men carrying their wands, the richly dressed Kavas — this is phonetic spelling, like most of mine — on the box with the driver, the latter generally in European dress, while the occupants display as much lace and as striking costumes as one would see in New York or Paris, is to see a common but constant sight and to add one more joy to the supreme delight of sojourning in the land of the

FIGURE 4. Letter from John Boyd Thacher to Will H. Low, March 1, 1889, Cairo, Egypt. AIHA, Gift of Alan Goldberg in honor of Phoebe Powell Bender and Matthew Bender, IV, LIB 2003.169.004.

for the museum. According to an article in the Albany newspaper *The Argus* for June 13, 1909, the Browns promised they would try to secure some Egyptian materials for the Albany Historical Society. While in Cairo, they stayed at the Eden Palace Hotel (figure 5) and received several letters from museum officials encouraging them to acquire Egyptian curios. Egyptian mummies were popular with the public, and according to the article in *The Argus*, "universally the first question a visitor asks when visiting a museum, please show us a mummy."[5]

In 1909, Brown wrote to Cuyler Reynolds, then the curator of the Albany Institute, about the cost of acquiring the mummies and coffins from the Egyptian Museum in Cairo for Albany (figure 6). An exhaustive search of Albany Institute records has yet to reveal the price Brown paid for the mummies and coffins.

> I am at a loss to understand why you should expect to get any of the Museum Curios for nothing. The Museum is a Government affair and everything going out of the Museum must be paid for at a fixed price whether for a museum or a private collection. These people are not in the Museum business for their health.[6]

Fortunately for Brown and the Albany Institute, the Egyptian Museum in Cairo (figures 7

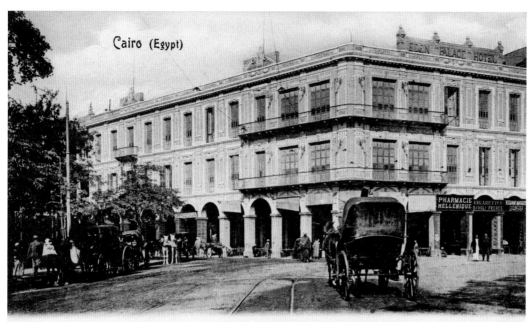

FIGURE 5. Postcard of Eden Palace Hotel, Cairo, ca. 1910. AIHA, LIB 2011.196.3.

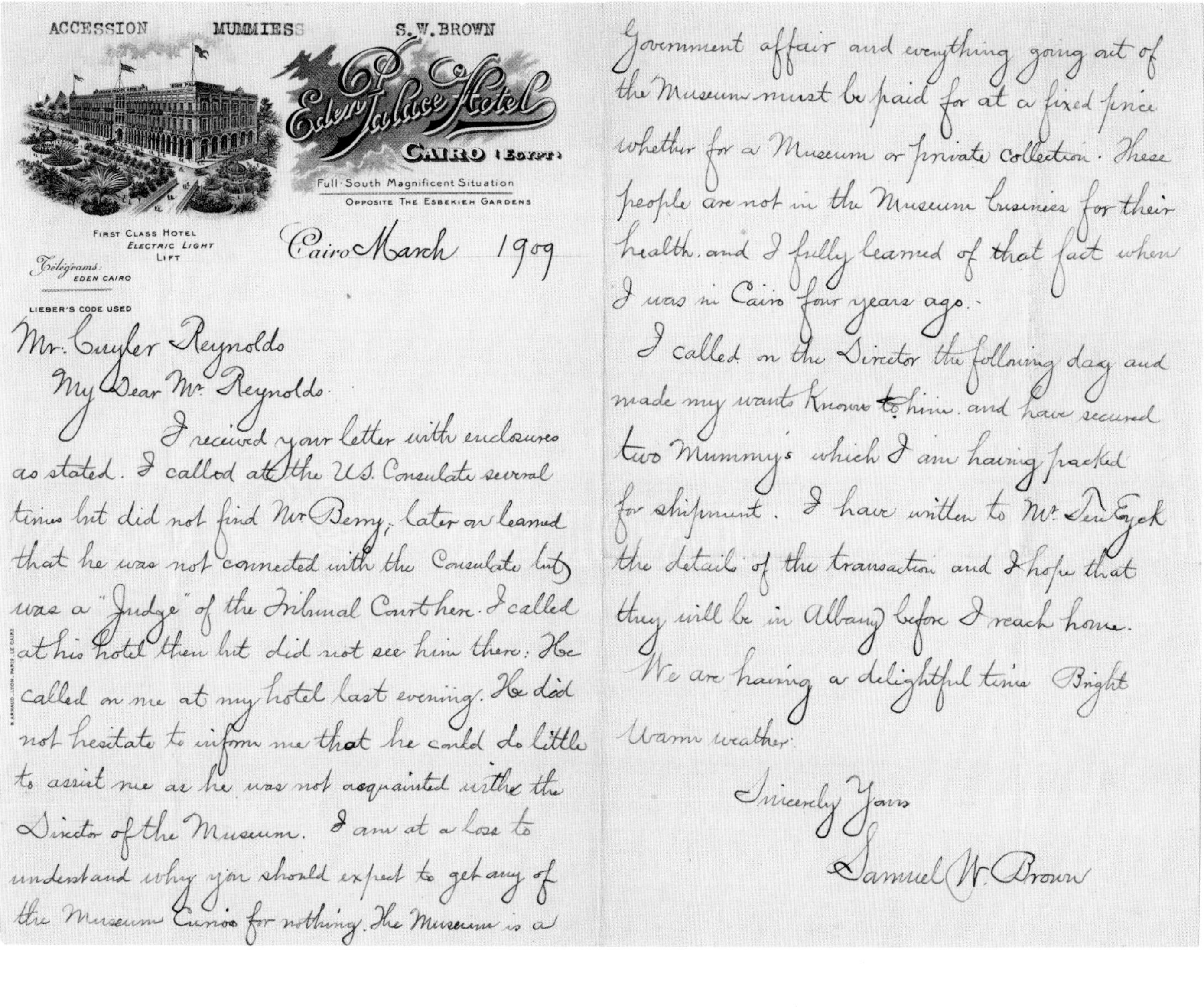

ACCESSION MUMMIES S. W. BROWN

Eden Palace Hotel
CAIRO (EGYPT)
Full South Magnificent Situation
Opposite The Esbekieh Gardens

First Class Hotel
Electric Light
Lift

Telegrams: EDEN CAIRO

LIEBER'S CODE USED

Cairo March 1909

Mr. Cuyler Reynolds

My Dear Mr. Reynolds

I received your letter with enclosures as stated. I called at the U.S. Consulate several times but did not find Mr Berry, later on learned that he was not connected with the Consulate but was a "Judge" of the Tribunal Court here. I called at his hotel then but did not see him there. He called on me at my hotel last evening. He did not hesitate to inform me that he could do little to assist me as he was not acquainted with the Director of the Museum. I am at a loss to understand why you should expect to get any of the Museum Curios for nothing. The Museum is a Government affair and everything going out of the Museum must be paid for at a fixed price whether for a Museum or private collection. These people are not in the Museum business for their health, and I fully learned of that fact when I was in Cairo four years ago.

I called on the Director the following day and made my wants known to him, and have secured two Mummy's which I am having packed for shipment. I have written to Mr. Ten Eyck the details of the transaction and I hope that they will be in Albany before I reach home.

We are having a delightful time Bright Warm weather.

Sincerely Yours

Samuel W. Brown

FIGURE 6. Letter from Samuel W. Brown to Cuyler Reynolds, March 1909, Cairo, Egypt. AIHA, LIB 2007.148_ms-002381.

CAIRO - The Egyptian Museum.

FIGURE 7. Postcard of the
Egyptian Museum, Cairo,
ca. 1909. Private collection.

and 8) was selling mummies to educational institutions in 1909, many from a cache discovered at Deir el-Bahri, later known as the Bab el-Gasus. A May 9, 1909, newspaper article, "Seen by an Albanian in Turkey and Egypt: Samuel Brown Brings Back Two Mummies for the Historical Society" (figure 9),[7] refers to Brown as an Albanian (denoting a person from Albany) and talks about his visit to Turkey before traveling to Egypt, describing in detail the mummies he purchased. The article also highlights the tombs at Amon, the ruins at Karnak, the pyramids, and the Sphinx. According to the 1909 *Argus* article:

> Mr. Brown selected two mummies, a man and a woman, instructing the assistant director to uncover the man

partly in order to allow him to see what condition he was in. Mr. Brown and his wife seated themselves beside the mummies while one of the employees went to work at it with his tools. He slashed the cloth which bound the head until he had reached the skull and as it proved to be hard the purchaser was delighted.

> The cloth has been cut through with a sharp knife directly at the center of the body, leaving the upper portion entirely stripped. This allows the visitor to see the innumerable windings of the bandage.[8]

The two mummies, described by the Egyptian Museum as a priest and priestess, left

Cairo via Suez on the steamship *Oceana* on March 11 and arrived in New York on April 22, 1909. From New York they traveled to Albany aboard the People's Line and were installed in the institute in new, specially built cases that were made in Rochester (figure 10).

Interest regarding these mummies remained high in Albany. In 1916 Miss A. M. Knapp wrote Brown to inquire why he did not bring back the coffin lid for the priestess and the coffin base for the "Reverend Highness." Brown replied that the lid and base were in a "decayed condition," persuading him to leave them at the museum. He described the lid of the Ptolemaic mummy as "being finely decorated not only with hieroglyphs, but a fairly large portrait in fine colors of his Reverend Highness" (figure 11).[9]

SAMUEL W. BROWN: THE MAN WHO BOUGHT THE ALBANY MUMMIES

Samuel Winfield Brown (1857–1940, figure 12) was born in New York City on November 5, 1857, and moved to Albany in 1874 to work as the bookkeeper for the Hope Banking Co. Three years later he took the job as bookkeeper for L. A. Chase & Co. (founded in 1833), which was a forerunner of the well-known wholesalers Bacon, Stickney & Co. Bacon joined the partnership in 1853, and in 1865, the name was changed to Bacon,

THE SUNDAY PRESS, MAY 9.

SEEN BY AN ALBANIAN IN TURKEY AND EGYPT

Samuel W. Brown Brings Back Two Mummies for the Historical Society—Witnessed Next to the Final Selamlik in Constantinople.

Two Egyptian mummies will soon be on exhibition at the Historical Society's building which have been presented by Samuel W. Brown, of the firm of Bacon, Stickney & Co., of this city. Mr. Brown has recently returned from a trip to Egypt, Turkey and the Holy Land. Mr. Brown was in Turkey the week before the last revolution broke out that resulted in the deposition of Sultan Abdul Hamid. While Mr. Brown did not see any evidences of the impending revolution, yet there was a feeling of uncertainty manifest everywhere. The passport issued to him by the Turkish government was not recognized for him to leave the country and he had to get his American passport endorsed by the American ambassador and then he was allowed to depart. When shown the Turkish passport the officials would say that "it is all right to-day, but maybe not to-morrow."

The Selamlik.

While in Constantinople, Mr. Brown had the privilege of witnessing the next to the final selamlik of the deposed sultan. This is the ceremony incident to the visit of the head of the faithful to the mosque to say his prayers. For centuries this custom has been followed in the same way. The new sultan, with the new order of things, has given up the custom and it is not expected to be seen in the Sublime Porte again. But one other has been held since the one witnessed by Mr. Brown. They have been held at noon on Fridays for centuries.

"On this occasion the sultan sat in the first carriage alone," said Mr. Brown. "In others following were seven of his wives, several of the young princes, eunuchs, priests and members of the cabinet. Before the start of the procession 8,000 troops, consisting of lancers, infantry and artillery, were drawn up on either side of the street leaving a narrow passageway through the lines for the procession. When he reaches the mosque a priest goes up in the minaret and calls the people to prayer. It would be more correct to say the soldiers, for the people are not permitted to take any part in the affair. There is a square where they are allowed to congregate to see the ruler, but iron railings are placed before them and in front of this solid rows of soldiers. After the announcement of the priest, no move is made by the soldiers or those within the mosque. Stillness reigns supreme, the whole making a beautiful picture. The bright uniforms of the soldiers and the red fez above all add a touch of color to the silent groups. When the sultan emerges, all is animation, the bands strike up into martial music, the soldiers cheer and the sultan stands in his carriage leaning on his sword with his left hand and with the other bows and mechanically waves it like a pump handle as he rides along without looking at his subjects. The devotions continue for a half hour, which the American joker would say "was a mighty short time for a man to pray who has as much to answer for as this wily old ex-autocrat. The grand vizier and a prince ride with him on his return to the palace. Foreigners are given an advantageous place to see the procession and admittance is arranged by the ambassador."

Land of the Nile.

From Turkey Mr. Brown went to Egypt. At the National Museum at Cairo he purchased two mummies, a man and a woman, which he has presented to the Historical Society of this city. The remains of the man are in an excellent state of preservation. The swathing has been cut off to the waist and removed, revealing the body of the ancient Egyptian. "The cloth was most of it in an excellent state of preservation," said Mr. Brown. "It is unbleached linen of about as fine texture as is produced to-day. Underneath the head was a piece of about half a yard which was found folded. It has a hemstitched edge and the piece is entire and strong. The gum arabic with the pieces added to it to preserve the body is first placed over the person about to be transformed into what the present irreverent age calls a mummy, then the wrapping begins. It is estimated that there were about 200 thicknesses of the cloth on the one obtained by Mr. Brown. Over the outer wrappings a sort of tar preparation is placed and then it is placed in a wooden coffin. The coffin is sealed tightly and the whole is then covered with a sort of plaster on which hieroglyphics are painted. The flesh has shrunken somewhat and is as hard as rock. The finger and toe nails are as perfect as when worn by the living. They are stained yellow with the juice of the henna plant after death. The form of the man is about five feet, eight inches tall and in life would weigh about 150 pounds. The head has a high forehead, denoting that this people were far removed from prehistoric man. A peculiarity noticed is that the middle toe is longer than the great toe. Anatomists contend that this should be so in the perfectly formed man. As the majority of the human race of this age are not so formed, the Egyptians undoubtedly were a more perfectly formed race than modern man. The body of the woman will not be unwrapped but will remain in her coffin as she was laid away. The men are mumified with the arms crossed over the breast, while the women have the arms by the side of the body. The coffin in which the woman was found is a fine specimen of the painting and writing of the Egyptian art. There are about a dozen pictures of the gods, with animals' heads and smaller animals, fishes, reptiles, implements and articles of common use on the sides of the coffin."

Mr. Brown has the key which was discovered about fifty years ago and it is his intention to decipher the inscriptions. Both bodies were buried about 966 B. C. and belonged to the twenty-second dynasty.

Tombs of Amon.

Both bodies were found in the tombs of the priests of Amon, near the ruins of the temple of Der-El-Badai, near Thebes, Egypt, 450 miles up the Nile on the western side of the river. The man was undoubtedly a high priest and the woman a high priestess, as the priests were buried in separate tombs and kings and officers in others. The tomb is in a sandstone mountain, with a low passageway leading into it from the surface. This was buried in the sand and was not discovered until 1820. This narrow way led further into the mountain, where it opened into broader avenues, and other passages opened at the sides into large rooms. These were all hewed out of the hard, solid rock. Where the mummy was found was a room at the end, 500 feet from the entrance and 150 feet below the surface. The amount of labor and time taken to construct the tomb may be judged from an incident that occurred several years ago. An American tourist succeeded in getting into the tomb unobserved and set to work with hammer and chisel to cut out a bas relief of a king on the walls. He worked until tired out and gave up the job. His efforts on the hard rock made so little impression that it can hardly be noticed. What tools the workers of those ancient days used to form the long passages and large rooms remains one of the mysteries of the land of the Nile. The rooms are covered with bas reliefs of the kings and hieroglyphics and paintings, which look as fresh as if the hand of time had known them not. The tomb was built in 1700 B. C., in the eighteenth dynasty.

Ruins of Karnak.

The tombs of Amon are near the ruins of the temple of Karnak, said to be the finest ruins in the world. A mountain of rock was selected for the temple and the magnificent temple was built out of it. The whole was cut away, leaving the walls and columns standing. Its construction was begun 1700 B. C and it was not completed until 1170 B. C. Each king in succession took up the work of building and the work progressed for over five centuries. In the center stands the grand hall of columns. There are 122 standing, 400 feet high and 27 feet in circumference. There were two obelisks standing in the temple, one of which was moved to Paris and the other remains. It has been pronounced the finest in Egypt. It is 98 feet in height. The temple was buried in the shifting sands of the desert and is not yet entirely excavated. The temple of Luxor was built of granite two miles from the temple of Karnak, and the two were connected by a paved way, lined on either side with a sphinx with a ram's head. The temple was built 1500 B. C. and was 500 feet long and 180 feet wide. It contains fourteen statues of Rhameses the Great.

FIGURE 9. "Seen by an Albanian in Turkey and Egypt: Samuel Brown Brings Back Two Mummies For the Historical Society," *Sunday Press*, May 9, 1909. AIHA, Museum Scrapbook Collection, 9.1.12, p. 131.

FIGURE 10. Egyptian mummies installed at the Albany Institute, ca. 1926. Photograph by Fellowcrafts Photo Studio. AIHA, Main Photo Collection, Series 52.

FIGURE 11. Letter from Samuel W. Brown to A. M. Knapp, March 7, 1916, Albany, NY. AIHA, LIB ms-002187.

ESTABLISHED 1834

Bacon, Stickney & Co.

COFFEES. SPICES. TEAS. ETC.
ALBANY. N.Y.

March 7th. 1916

Miss. A,M. Knapp.

Dear Madam:-

I have your letter of the 6th. inst. and replying to same beg to say that I have seen the cover to the Mummy Case referred to only in fragments in the Museum in Cairo Egypt it being in so decayed a condition that it fell apart upon even careful handling so that I did not get another to take its place,preferring to have none rather than a substitute for the original. The same can be said of her friend the Reverend Highness across the way who is reposing on the cover of his house rather than in the house itsself which also fell apart when handled it being very badly decayed but the cover which is finely decorated not only with hieroglyphics but a fairly large portrait in fine colors of his Reverend Highness, was in good enough condition to bring him home on and to use in the exhibit.

I am sorry that I cannot comply with the request of Mr.Lansing for next sunday afternoon as I have a hospital meeting on hand. for that afternoon but will come the following sunday instead.

Very Respectfully. Samuel W Brown

FIGURE 12. Samuel W. Brown, ca. 1900. Unidentified photographer. AIHA, Albany Art Union Archive, MG 79. B113.F28.

Stickney & Co. The company's motto was "Good goods at fair prices, and honorable dealing to all, with the closest attention to business." Products included ginger, fabric dye, red pepper, coffee, allspice, baking powder, poultry seasoning, and a variety of other goods. (Note the Egyptian-stylized images on the Best Ginger Canister, figure 13.)

After his first wife, Sarah Owston, died in 1892, Brown married Rosa A. Stickney in 1902.

She was the widow of Milton W. Stickney (1852–1898), a partner in the company. Brown became president of Bacon, Stickney & Co. in 1925, a position he held until his death in 1940. During his lifetime, Brown was actively involved in the Albany community. He served as vestryman and treasurer of St. Peter's Episcopal Church, trustee and treasurer of Albany Memorial Hospital, a trustee of the Hudson River Humane Society, and a supporter of the Albany Association of the Blind. He was a member of the Master Lodge of Masons, the Clinton Lodge of Odd Fellows, the Albany Club, and the Albany Chamber of Commerce. In 1912, Brown became a trustee of the Albany Institute, a position he held for twenty-eight years. He is buried in Albany Rural Cemetery along with Rosa, who died in 1923.

THE ALBANY MUMMIES: FIRST ONE HUNDRED YEARS AT THE ALBANY INSTITUTE

Officials at the Egyptian Museum in Cairo told Samuel W. Brown that the 21st Dynasty mummy was a priestess and the Ptolemaic Period mummy was a man. Since their arrival in 1909, a number of Egyptologists, medical personnel, and scholars have examined the mummies and coffins with

surprising revelations. According to an article in *The Knickerbocker News* on January 29, 1941, two renowned Egyptologists visited the museum on two separate days to examine the Albany Mummies with institute director John Davis Hatch. Dr. Ludlow Bull, curator in Egyptology in the Metropolitan Museum of Art, and John Cooney, curator in Egyptology at the Brooklyn Museum, concluded that the 21st Dynasty mummy was a priest, not a priestess, because of the hieroglyphic inscriptions on the coffin.[10] Unfortunately, this new scholarship was not added to the curatorial files, nor were the display labels changed to reflect this revelation. In 1961, a similar event occurred. The two mummies were X-rayed, and a newspaper article in the *Sunday Times Union* on January 22, 1961, revealed that both mummies were male. Again, this new information was never added to the curatorial files, nor were the labels changed. These articles were only recently rediscovered in 2013 in old publicity files.[11]

In 1988, Albany Medical Center conducted X-rays and CT scans of the mummies with the goal of looking for hidden amulets and jewelry, which did not exist as it turned out. The scans did reveal what appeared to be

FIGURE 13. "Best Ginger" spice canister, Bacon, Stickney & Co., Albany, NY, ca. 1890. AIHA, gift of Phoebe Bender, 1991.28.

an artificial toe on the 21st Dynasty mummy. The mummies were featured on the Learning Channel's 2003 program *Ancient ER*, in part because of the rare prosthetic toe. Also at this time, Bethyl Mayer, a graduate student at the State University of New York at Albany, who worked with Egyptologists to translate the hieroglyphs on the 21st Dynasty coffin, determined that the mummy board was in the collection of the British Museum in London and the coffin lid was owned by the Kunsthistoriches Museum in Vienna.

THE ALBANY MUMMIES TODAY: INTERSECTION OF SCHOLARSHIP, SCIENCE, AND TECHNOLOGY

Dr. Peter Lacovara, retired senior curator of ancient Egyptian, Nubian, and Near Eastern art at the Michael C. Carlos Museum, Emory University, resolved the first mystery of the

Albany Mummies by accurately dating both mummies and coffins using current scholarship. Not long after he moved to Albany in 2007, Lacovara began working with Albany

Institute staff on the installation of its Ancient Egyptian Gallery. Like previous scholars, Lacovara concluded from the hieroglyphs that the coffin belonged to Ankhefenmut, a sculptor and priest in the Temple of Mut, who lived between 1069 and 945 BC. He confirmed that the mummy board of the museum's elaborately decorated 21st Dynasty coffin base is in London, and the coffin lid is in Vienna. At this time Lacovara proposed that AIHA mount a major exhibition to reunite the parts of Ankhefenmut's coffin and highlight how and why the Egyptian Museum in Cairo presented the coffin lid to the Kunsthistorisches Museum in 1893 and the mummy board to the British Museum in 1903 as gifts of the Egyptian government.

Lacovara also noted the unwrapped Ptolemaic mummy was resting in the 21st Dynasty coffin, and the 21st Dynasty mummy was resting in the Ptolemaic Period coffin, which led to further confusion about the sex and identification of the mummies. When they first arrived in Albany from Egypt in 1909, each was in its proper coffin. The 21st Dynasty mummy, identified by the Cairo Museum as a female, arrived in a 21st Dynasty coffin bottom inscribed with the owner's name, Ankhefenmut.

This early identification of the mummy as female precluded her from being the male priest Ankhefenmut. The Ptolemaic Period mummy, identified as a male priest by the Cairo Museum, arrived in an unmarked Ptolemaic Period coffin base. Little is known about this mummy's identity, because Brown left the coffin lid at the Cairo Museum due to its badly damaged condition. If this coffin lid came to Albany, the identity of the priest could be determined from the inscription on the coffin.

In preparation for the exhibition, Lacovara recommended a thorough reexamination of both mummies with the primary objective of determining their sex and age at death. He was hopeful that the 21st Dynasty mummy could actually be male and therefore the priest and sculptor Ankhefenmut.

SCIENCE AND TECHNOLOGY

The second mystery, the identification of the sex of the 21st Dynasty mummy, was solved on March 31, 2012, when the Albany Institute's two mummies were transported to Albany Medical Center to be CT scanned and X-rayed. The 2012 team examining the mummies consisted of Lacovara and Dr. Bob Brier, who specializes in mummification; two Albany Medical Center radiologists, Dr. Phuong Vinh and Dr. Michael Schuster; a CT scan technician, Howard Mayforth; and X-ray technician Emily Johnson Chapin. The CT scans were done on a machine capable of images as thin as 0.6 mm, permitting high-resolution images.

To everyone's surprise and delight, the 21st Dynasty priestess turned out to be a male between fifty and fifty-five years old. (See "The Mummy of Ankhefenmut: a Scientific Investigation," p. 79.) The CT scans provided detailed pictures of its skeletal structure with decidedly male attributes—thicker, more robust, and angular bones in the pelvis, jaw, and brows. With the sex of the mummy determined as male, experts realized that he could be Ankhefenmut, the temple priest and sculptor. The male mummy's upper right side (most ancient Egyptians were right-handed) was decidedly more muscular than his left side, indicating that he spent much of his time in physical activity, perhaps repeatedly hefting a mallet and sending it crashing down on a chisel, as would have been necessary for sculpting statues.

The Ptolemaic mummy underwent the same examination. The sex of this mummy was confirmed to be male; he probably died in his forties and had a healthy diet. (See "The Ptolemaic Mummy: A Scientific Investigation," p. 101.)

NEW DISCOVERY

During a close examination of Ankhefenmut's mummy and coffin, several bundles and numerous loose pieces of linen were discovered underneath the mummy. Guided by Lacovara, textile conservator Patricia Ewer and two Albany textile specialists, Albany Institute board member Karen Nicholson and her colleague, Kathleen Munn, thoroughly examined the textiles, with surprising results.

They identified the materials through microscopic analysis, counted the threads, and photographed the materials. The largest bundle turned out to be a rare surviving example of a tunic or priest's robe. As the material was carefully unfolded, it revealed evidence of an armhole, neckline, belt holes, and decorative fringe at the bottom. Another large piece of fabric, possibly a shawl with blue indigo threads, was also discovered. (See essay, "Ankhefenmut's Tunic," p. 72).

The museum's collection of Egyptian antiquities began in the late nineteenth century with objects such as amulets, jewelry, and a section of the Book of the Dead. Today, the collection numbers over seventy objects. Early donors included Ellen Campbell, Theodore Davis, Sarah Paine Potter, John Townsend Lansing, and Samuel W. Brown. In 1989, Egyptologist Gerald Weinberg, professor of history emeritus at the University of North Carolina, Chapel Hill, donated a 21st Dynasty *shabti* (a funerary figurine) to the museum in honor of his parents. He credits his early visits to the museum when he lived in Albany in shaping his interest in ancient Egypt.

In 2005, Jane Bryant Quinn, in honor of David Conrad Quinn, donated a selection of books key to the study of ancient Egypt. The books included sixteen of the twenty volumes of Napoleon's *Description de l'Égypte* (1809–1828); a copy of Giovanni Battista Belzoni's *Narrative of the Operations and Recent Discoveries within the Pyramids, Temples, Tombs, and Excavations in Egypt and Nubia* (1821), and the accompanying volume, *Plates Illustrative of the Researches and Operations of G. Belzoni in Egypt and Nubia* (1821); Jean-François Champollion's celebrated 1824 book, *Précis du système hieroglyphique des anciens Égyptiens*, where he recounts the steps involved in deciphering the Rosetta Stone; and *Sir J. Gardner Wilkinson's Manners and Customs of the Ancient Egyptians* (1847). (See essay, "Egyptian Volumes at the Albany Institute," p. 24.)

In 2013, Dr. Heinrich Medicus of Troy, New York, donated thirty-two ancient Egyptian objects, almost doubling the museum's collection of Egyptian materials. Highlights include a stone head from an official from the New Kingdom, ca. 1400 BC, a rare bronze statuette of the goddess Mut, a head from a *shabti* of King Seti I, a relief carving from a temple built by Akhenaton and Nefertiti, and a lapis lazuli Akkadian cylinder seal from the world's first great empire. Today with additional donations from Mr. and Mrs. Arnold Cogswell, Peter Lacovara, Elaine Liuzzi, Alice M. Schrade, and others, the museum's collections have been greatly enhanced. See page 107 for an illustrated checklist of AIHA collections.

Since 1909, the Albany Mummies have been on continuous exhibition in multiple galleries throughout the museum. We will continue to collect ancient Egyptian materials to enhance the story of the Albany Mummies and delight visitors of all ages.

NOTES

1. Child's *Albany City Directory*, 1831.

2. *The Egyptian Pantheon: An Explanatory Catalogue of Egyptian Antiquities, Collected and Classified with Especial Reference to the Religion and Funerary Rites of Ancient Egypt, by Armand de Potter, and Exhibited in the Egyptian Section of the Archaeological Department in the Anthropological Building, World's Columbian Exposition, Chicago, U.S.A.* (New York, 1893).

3. J. F. Romano, "The Armand de Potter Collection of Ancient Egyptian Art," in *Studies in Honor of William Kelly Simpson*, vol. 2, ed. P. Der Manuelian (Boston, 1996), 697–711.

4. Letter written by John Boyd Thacher to Will H. Low from Cairo, Egypt, March 1, 1889, AIHA Library Collection, 2003.169.004.

5. "Egyptian Mummies Now on Exhibition," *Argus*, June 13, 1909, AIHA, MG 246.

6. Letter written by Samuel Brown to Cuyler Reynolds from Cairo, Egypt, March 1909, AIHA Library Collection, 2007.148.MS-002381.

7. *Sunday Press*, May 9, 1909, AIHA Library Collection, Museum Scrapbook Collection, 9.1.12, p. 131.

8. "Egyptian Mummies Now on Exhibition," *Argus*, June 13, 1909, AIHA Library Collection, MG246.

9. Letter from Samuel W. Brown to A. M. Knapp, March 7, 1916, Albany, NY, AIHA Library Collection, MG246.

10. "Experts Scan Mummies to Trace Lives," *Knickerbocker News*, January 29, 1941; "'Maid' at Art Institute 'Unmasked' as Male Priest," *Knickerbocker News*, January 29, 1941, AIHA, MG 246.

11. Michael Pilley, "Mummies an Enigma, Not Much Is Known About Them, But They're a Hit at Institute," *Sunday Times Union*, January 22, 1961, AIHA, MG 246.

Egyptomania and the Empire State

Peter Lacovara

Some of the first historical accounts of Egypt were given by the Greek historians Herodotus, Strabo, Diodorus Siculus, and the largely lost work of Manetho, an Egyptian priest during the reigns of Ptolemy I and Ptolemy II in the third century BC, who divided the history of Egypt into the dynastic system we use today. The Ptolemies were very interested in the work of their ancient predecessors, and they restored and enhanced many of the temples. They built many new temples and monuments in the Egyptian style. The Romans continued to build Egyptianizing monuments and even carried out restoration work on the Great Sphinx and Colossi of Memnon.

The age of the pharaohs fascinated Muslim scholars, such as Abdul Latif al-Baghdadi, a teacher at Cairo's Al-Azhar University in the thirteenth century who wrote detailed descriptions of ancient Egyptian monuments, as did the famous historian al-Maqriz (1364–1442). Early European travel accounts of Egypt concentrated on the mystical, with many fanciful and inaccurate renderings of the ruins. More accurate records were published by later scholars (Claude Sicard, Benoît de Maillet, Frederic Louis Norden, and Richard Pococke). The first serious attempt at precise recording was undertaken in the early seventeenth century by John Greaves, who measured the pyramids and published them in his *Pyramidographia*. The Jesuit priest/scientist Athanasius Kircher was perhaps the first to hint at the phonetic value of the mysterious hieroglyphs, suggesting that Coptic, the liturgical language of the Orthodox Egyptian Church, was a vestige of the ancient Egyptian language.

The field of Egyptology was truly born in the late eighteenth century with the French invasion of Egypt in 1798. Along with his soldiers, Napoleon brought scholars and artists to record the monuments, artifacts, flora, fauna, and art and architecture they encountered. These were published in a massive series of folio volumes, the *Description de l'Égypte*, between 1809 and 1828 (figure 14; see "Egyptian Volumes in the Albany Institute" for these and other volumes). The incredibly accurate plates that illustrated the folios were an invaluable tool for scholars and came to serve as pattern books for artists, architects, and artisans. The vogue for everything Egyptian created by these books ignited the first global wave of Egyptomania and manifested itself along with ancient Greek and Roman design in the empire style.

New York architect Ithiel Town added a set of the *Description* volumes to his famed library, and his partner, Alexander Jackson Davis, was inspired to create a number of designs for Egyptian-style buildings, including one for consideration for the Halls of Justice in New York City. Another Egyptianizing design won the competition for that building. The designer, by John Haviland, was also inspired by the *Description*, and the prison earned the nickname "The Tombs."

Although found by the French expedition and published in the *Description*, an inscribed fragment known as the Rosetta Stone was part of the spoils of war that the Duke of Wellington claimed after Napoleon's defeat. It was presented to the British Museum in 1802, but it was not until 1822 that a French linguist, Jean-François Champollion, was able to decipher the hieroglyphs on it by comparing them to a translation of the inscription written in Greek below (see "Egyptian Volumes"). The translation caused a sensation, and a U.S. version was soon published by the student literary Philomathean Society in Philadelphia in 1858.

Inspired by the success of the *Description*, a number of other expeditions set out to record the monuments, including a Franco-Italian mission headed by Champollion and a German one. An enterprising Buffalo publisher, Samuel Augustus Binion, drew on a number of these different sets to produce his own version, which included some original reconstructions, titled *Ancient Egypt*, or *Mizraim*.

There was great interest not only in copying the antiquities but in bringing them back to the West. Museum representatives and wealthy individuals went to Egypt or hired agents to collect for them. One of the most

successful, and certainly the most colorful, was an Italian circus strongman named Giovanni Belzoni. Belzoni made some of the most spectacular archaeological discoveries of all time, including the great temple of Abu Simbel and the beautiful tomb of Seti I in the Valley of the Kings. A born showman, Belzoni cleverly marketed his discoveries by displaying a replica of Seti's tomb in London and publishing thrilling accounts of his finds.

Statues, stelae, and other artifacts were exported in great quantity from the land of the pharaohs, but no artifacts created as much interest as did mummies and coffins. The care with which the ancient Egyptians preserved their dead was a source of endless fascination. In the early nineteenth century, a number of enterprising showmen toured mummies around the country, taking them out of their coffins and unwrapping them for a paying audience. One tour came to Rensselaerville, New York (twenty-four miles south of Albany) in 1828. Unfortunately, a group of students broke in to the venue, and in trying to examine the mummy wound up destroying it. Another mummy, that of Padihershef, which belonged to the Massachusetts General Hospital, was sent on a tour of the Northeast and was displayed in the

old New York State Capitol building in 1824. A beautiful nested set of coffins without a mummy and a fine Egyptian collection were presented to the Troy Public Library in 1902, but that collection was dispersed at auction in 1973.

Since the days of the Romans, the most spectacular prize that could be wrested from the banks of the Nile was an obelisk. After the Roman emperors took back more than a dozen to Rome and Istanbul, the European powers sought to follow in their footsteps, with the French taking one obelisk from the front of Luxor Temple and transplanting it to the Place de la Concorde in 1836, followed by

FIGURE 14. Plate 3, "Memphis. Vue des ruines, prise du sudest," from *Description de l'Égypte pendant l'expédition de l'armée française*, vol. 5 (1822) detail. AIHA, gift of Jane Bryant Quinn in honor of David Conrad Quinn, LIB 2005.144 [WU1].9. This plate shows Napoleon's *savants* measuring a colossal hand in the ruins of Memphis, with the pyramids of Giza in the background.

the British, who erected one along the banks of the Thames in 1878.

Not to be outdone, the Americans felt it was their turn, as newspapers recounted the excitement surrounding the shipment and erection of the London obelisk. New York City Park commissioners began planning and fundraising for that project, which was soon championed by the likes of William H.

Vanderbilt and Frederic Church (figure 15). A fallen obelisk in red granite almost 70 feet tall and weighing 240 tons, carved in the reign of Thutmosis III (c. 1479–1425 BC) and reinscribed by Ramesses II (c. 1279–1213 BC) was selected. This was the mate to the London obelisk; both had been discovered in Alexandria. The pair had originally been set up in the temple at Heliopolis but were later transported to the Delta in the reign of Cleopatra VII, which earned them the popular appellation of Cleopatra's Needles.

The task of moving the monolith to New York was given to U.S. Navy Lieutenant Commander Henry Gorringe, who cleverly loaded it into a ship's hold by sliding it on top of rolling cannon balls. After the monolith arrived in New York, it took thirty-two horses hitched together to haul it from the banks of the Hudson River to Central Park. A special railroad bridge and steam engine were required to bring it through the park and set it up on a small rise overlooking the new Metropolitan Museum of Art. The cornerstone for the obelisk was set in place by none other than the Grand Master of Masons of the State of New York, on October 2, 1880, with more than 9,000 Masons parading up Fifth Avenue for the ceremony.

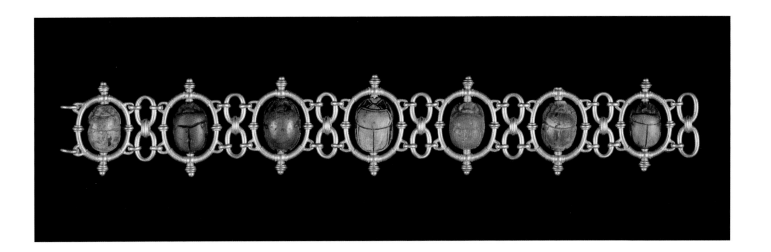

The ancient society of the Fraternal Order of the Masons traces its roots to medieval guilds of stone masons, and some say even further back, associating the organization to pharaonic Egypt. Egyptian revival design is a feature of many Masonic lodges and symbols, including the "eye of providence" found on the back of the U.S. one-dollar bill. The costumes worn by the Masons included fezzes embroidered with Egyptian motifs and names of place names like Karnak and Luxor.

Egyptian costume and jewelry enjoyed great popularity for all classes of the public in the nineteenth and early twentieth centuries. Tiffany & Company incorporated many Egyptian designs in their work and sometimes included genuine Egyptian artifacts. Scarabs, small oval-shaped gems in the shape of beetles that symbolized resurrection to the ancient Egyptians, were the most popular (figure 16), and Tiffany issued a number of scarabs in its signature iridescent glass. Egyptian designs were also used in many decorative household items, such as Oneida flatware.

People took an interest in visiting Egypt, and increasing numbers of tourists traveled down the Nile. The English novelist Amelia Edwards's *A Thousand Miles Up the Nile* was a best-selling travelogue, and her concern for the destruction of ancient sites led to the founding of the Egypt Exploration Fund (now Society, EES). The society had English and U.S. supporters, including Albanian George Douglas Miller, who was honorary secretary of the EES from 1889 to 1894. Through the work of its excavators, including the great Sir William Matthew Flinders Petrie, the EES shared many of its finds with museums in New York and New England.

Museums were also able to acquire objects by purchasing them directly from Egypt, and the Cairo Museum had a special salesroom to sell off duplicates of its vast holdings. This is where Samuel Brown went to make his acquisitions for the Albany Institute of History & Art.

FIGURE 16. Bracelet made of ancient scarabs in a Victorian gold setting. New Kingdom to Late Period, ca. 1550–664 BC, probably French mount, ca. 1870. Gold, Egyptian faience, and glazed steatite. AIHA, gift of John Townsend Lansing, 1900.7.1. Genuine scarabs were used in this Victorian bracelet.

Andrew Oliver

One of the most remarkable publishing initiatives of the nineteenth century—matched only by Alexander von Humboldt's multivolume work on the New World, which appeared about the same time—is the series of volumes published in Paris by a specially established commission to record the work of the 150 artists and scientists—the *savants*—taken to Egypt by Napoleon on his ill-fated effort to seize the country to counteract British influence in the East. Covering Egypt's antiquities, its contemporary state, and its natural history, the *Description de l'Égypte* (figure 17) was published in installments—the dates of the volumes range from 1809 to 1828—the text is in small folio, the plates are in large folio, making twenty-three volumes in all.

In 2005, AIHA received a gift of seventeen volumes of the first edition (in the second edition, the text is in twenty-five volumes in octavo format, and no plates are colored). The institute's set lacks selected volumes of *État moderne* and *Histoire naturelle*, but fortunately contains all of the text and plate volumes devoted to *Antiquités*. The volumes retain their original bindings—red leather spines, red paper-covered board with gilded fleur-de-lis borders typical of the Paris binder Jean-Joseph Tessier.

U.S. libraries and architects displayed an early interest in the *Description de l'Égypte*. The first set to reach the United States was given to Harvard College Library in 1826 by a graduate of the college. In the late 1820s and 1830s, several architects in New York and Philadelphia purchased sets to draw upon the plates depicting ancient ruins for their designs of what became known as Egyptian Revival architecture. This style took its place alongside Gothic and Classical Revival styles, but in the end was not favored for houses, churches, or civic buildings freely visited by the public, instead reserved for the façades of prisons and the entrance gates to cemeteries, structures evoking eternity.

At the same time, in the 1830s and 1840s, libraries such as the American Philosophical Society in Philadelphia, the Providence Athenaeum, the Boston Athenaeum, and the New York Society Library purchased sets of the *Description* as

works essential for their patrons—libraries where these volumes can still be con-
sulted. Select universities, such as Princ-
eton, Brown, Yale, and South Carolina
College in Columbia, acquired sets by gift
or purchase. Last, any number of wealthy
people, taking advantage of sets offered by
booksellers and at auctions in New York,
Boston, and Philadelphia, acquired the
work as trophies for their private libraries.

The set in the Albany Institute is not
the first to reach the city. In the mid-
1840s, a French entrepreneur, Alexandre

Vattemare, arranged for exchanges of publications between French and U.S. institutions. Among the works he brought and
presented to U.S. libraries were three sets
of the *Description de l'Égypte*. One set went
to the National Institute of Washington for
the Promotion of Science and the Useful
Arts, a second went to the North Carolina
State Library in Raleigh, and the third went
to the State Library of New York in Albany.
The set sent to Washington was later transferred to the Library of Congress where,
as a duplicate, it was ultimately discarded.

FIGURE 17. Frontispiece and
title page of the first plate
volume of the *Description de
l'Égypte* (Paris, 1809). Etching
and engraving by Abraham
Girardet and François Noël Sel-
lier after a drawing by François-
Charles Cécile. Composite view
of Egyptian monuments, framed
by allusions to the Napoleonic
campaign. AIHA, gift of Jane
Bryant Quinn in honor of David
Conrad Quinn, LIB 2005.144.5.

The set sent to Raleigh was transferred to the University of North Carolina at Chapel Hill, and the set presented to Albany was lost in March 1911 when the State Library burned down. In 1920, the State Library acquired a replacement set of the *Description*, a set once owned by the New York Public Library, sold at auction as a duplicate. It had come to the New York Public Library in 1908 as the bequest of Matilda Wolfe Bruce, who had inherited it from her father, George Bruce, a leading New York type founder, who had purchased it at auction in 1840.

In the decade after Napoleon's invasion of Egypt and then defeat by the British, an Ottoman officer, Mehemet Ali, became the sole ruler of Egypt. With the help of expatriate Europeans, he transformed the country's economy and its military and civil institutions (at least for the upper classes), and he welcomed Europeans interested in its history. Several of the consuls stationed in Egypt actively began to collect antiquities, employing adventurous Europeans to work on their behalf; two were notable: Bernadino Drovetti, Italian-born French consul from 1803 to 1815, and 1821 to 1829; and Henry Salt, British consul from 1816

to 1827. Drovetti employed Jean-Jacques Rifaud (among others), who came to Egypt in 1814 and excavated dozens of significant sculptures and other antiquities at Thebes and elsewhere on the Nile. Salt employed Giovanni Battista Belzoni, an Italian-born strongman who had performed in the circus before coming to Egypt in 1815. He was active until 1819, working at the pyramids of Giza, at Abu Simbel, and in the tombs of the kings at Thebes, where he opened the tomb of Pharaoh Seti I, perhaps his most significant discovery. Rifaud and Belzoni produced publications of their activities. Among the works on Egypt acquired by the Albany Institute is a copy of Belzoni's work, *Narrative of the Operations and Recent Discoveries within the Pyramids, Temples, Tombs, and Excavations in Egypt and Nubia* (second edition of 1821) with the accompanying folio volume, *Plates Illustrative of the Researches and Operations of G. Belzoni in Egypt and Nubia* (figures 18 and 19). The volumes bear the bookplates of the nineteenth-century London banker Henry Christopher Robarts (1811–1890).

During this period, with rising interest in Egyptian antiquities, several European scholars sought to decipher hieroglyphs.

Two in particular were preeminent: the Englishman Thomas Young and the Frenchman Jean-François Champollion. The bilingual inscription from the Rosetta Stone, in hieroglyphic, demotic, and Greek scripts (found in 1799 by the French who had come with Napoleon, but seized in 1801 by the British after bitter negotiations) was one of the keys. Before surrendering the stone, the French had made lithographic impressions of it (the signs reproduced in reverse), which came to France. Once the stone was in London, plaster casts were made available to learned institutions, including the Bibliothèque nationale in Paris. With help from various sources (including Young), not all of it acknowledged, Champollion succeeded in his quest and is credited with deciphering the hieroglyphs. In 1822, he read a paper before the Académie des Inscriptions et Belles-Lettres—a session attended by Alexander von Humboldt and Thomas Young—soon published as *Lettre à M. Dacier, secrétaire perpétual de l'Académie royale des inscriptions et belles-lettres, relative à l'alphabet des hieroglyphs phonetiques*, in which he announced his breakthrough, and in 1824 he issued his definitive *Précis du système hiéroglyphique des anciens Égyptiens*, in which he demonstrated conclusively that he had deciphered hieroglyphic script. A copy of this celebrated 1824 work has also come to the Albany Institute.

Champollion's work in the 1820s allowed hieroglyphic signs to be read, which brought a new understanding to Egyptian history. Champollion was significant in another respect. In 1826, he persuaded French King Charles X to open galleries in the Louvre for the exhibition of Egyptian antiquities, where his first task as curator was the acquisition of a collection of Egyptian antiquities formed by British consul Henry Salt. But Champollion had never been to Egypt. He and an Italian colleague, Ippolito Rosellini, backed by royal and private patrons, organized a joint French-Tuscan expedition to explore the ruins of Egypt. In August 1828, accompanied by an architect and four artists, Champollion reached Alexandria, where he joined Rosellini, who had likewise brought along an architect and artists. After going as far south as Wadi Halfa on the Nile, the teams lived at Thebes for six months and left Egypt at the end of 1829.

In 1831, they issued a prospectus advertising a joint publication, but Champollion died unexpectedly in 1832, and his brother was unable to come to an agreement with Rosellini. As a result, Rosellini published his own account of their joint expedition, *I Monumenti dell'Egitto e della Nubia*, with nine volumes of text in octavo and three volumes of plates in folio (the last text volume and final set of plates appearing in 1844, a year after Rosellini's death), and Champollion's brother issued a separate

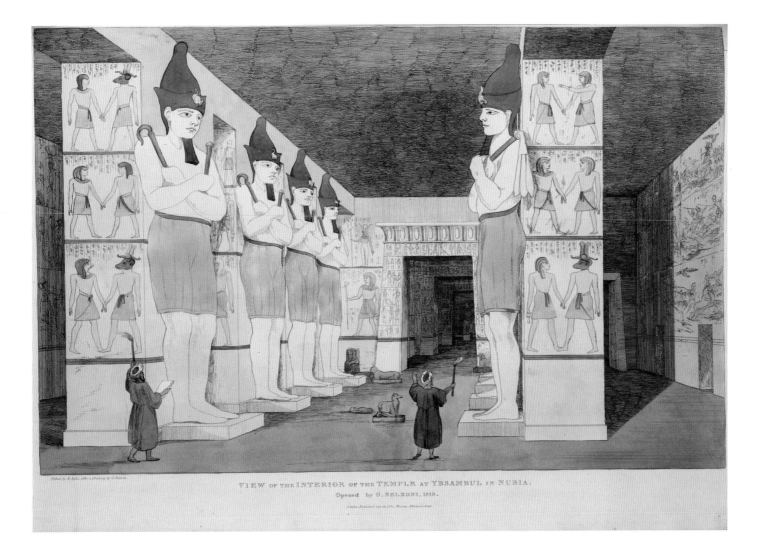

VIEW OF THE INTERIOR OF THE TEMPLE AT YBSAMBUL IN NUBIA.
Opened by G. BELZONI, 1818.

version in four folio volumes (the text volumes were never written), which appeared from 1835 to 1845, with the same title, but in French, *Monuments de l'Égypte et de la Nubie*. A set of Champollion's magnificent plate volumes has also come to the Albany Institute to further enhance its important collection of early volumes on the exploration of the Nile Valley and its civilizations.

FIGURE 19. Plate 43, "View of the Interior of the Temple at Ybsambul in Nubia. Opened by G. Belzoni, 1818," from *Plates Illustrative of the Researches and Operations of G. Belzoni in Egypt and Nubia* (London, 1822). After a drawing by Giovanni Belzoni. AIHA, gift of Jane Bryant Quinn in honor of David Conrad Quinn, LIB 2005.144.23.

Ankhefenmut and His World

Peter Lacovara and Joyce Haynes

Samuel Brown was fortunate in the timing of his shopping trip to the Cairo Museum. In 1891 a sealed tomb had been discovered in western Thebes, in front of the temple of Hatshepsut at Deir el-Bahri, which came to be known as the Bab el-Gasus ("the Gate of the Priests") (figure 20).[1] Reached through a large circular pit that had been covered by limestone slabs and mud bricks, the tomb was a huge catacomb cut in the rock nearly fifty feet below the surface. The shaft from the surface led to a corridor running about 300 feet in length, which led to a chamber and another side corridor (figure 21).[2] The corridors and main chamber were crammed floor to ceiling with coffins, boxes, baskets, canopic jars, statues, wooden stelae, and other funerary offerings. Fearing robbery by local bandits, the officials of the Egyptian Antiquities Service removed the contents of the cache for shipment to Cairo in just a week, with little recorded about the details of the burial.

One of the few accounts of the discovery is found in a newspaper report of the time:

> Here is some account of a fortunate discovery. Having found, *in situ*, at Deir-el-Bahari, a royal sarcophagus of a queen, and seeing that the surrounding ground had not been disturbed, I thought it worth while to make further excavations on the spot.
>
> At a depth of fifteen metres we came upon the door of a rock-cut chamber, in which were piled, one above the other, 180 mummy cases of priests and priestesses of Amen, together with a large number of the usual funerary objects, including

FIGURE 20. Deir el-Bahri. The tomb situated in front of the temple of Hatshepsut at Deir el-Bahri, and visible as a small circle in the center of this photograph, came to be known as the Bab el-Gasus ("the Gate of the Priests"). Reached through a large circular pit that had been hidden by limestone slabs and mud bricks, it was a vast catacomb cut in the rock nearly fifty feet below. Photograph courtesy of the Metropolitan Museum of Art.

some fifty Osirian statuettes. Of these we at once opened ten, finding a papyrus in each.

There are a great many enormous wooden sarcophagi, containing mummies in triple mummy cases, all very richly decorated. Among these we have found a priest of Aahhotep. These sarcophagi are of the time of the twenty-first dynasty. What we have found is therefore a "cache" of the same period as that of royal mummies discovered in 1881, and made by the same priests of Amen.

Notwithstanding that the soil has remained untouched for 3000 years some of these sarcophagi are broken and many of the gilded faces of the superincumbent effigies are injured. The way in which they are piled up, their damaged condition, and the general disorder, point to a hurried and wholesale removal, as in the case of the royal mummies. We find, for instance a mummy case inscribed with one name enclosed in a sarcophagus inscribed with another, while probably the inner cases may

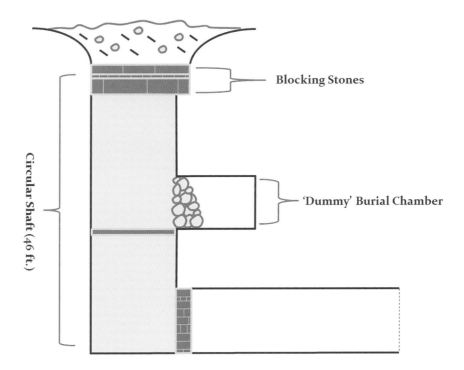

Circular Shaft (46 ft.)

Blocking Stones

'Dummy' Burial Chamber

FIGURE 21. Plan of the Bab el-Gasus cache tomb. The massive tomb used for the cache may have been constructed in the early New Kingdom and later adapted for the temple personnel of Karnak. Drawing by Daniel Warne.

prove to belong to a mummy with a name different from both. May we here hope to find some royal mummies for which there was not space in the vault discovered ten years ago? I scarcely dare to hope it.

At a first glance it would seem as if the high priests had abstained from burying the mummies of their more humble predecessors with those of royalty. Everything must, however, be opened and studied.

About midway of the shaft now open may be seen the door of an upper vault; and, to judge by certain indications, there is also, probably, an intermediate vault. Had we, however, only the 180 sarcophagi contemporary with, or anterior to, the 21st dynasty, it would be a magnificent haul, the greater number of the sarcophagi being really splendid and in perfect preservation. There are also some charming things among the minor objects.

The name has been purposely erased, or washed off, from several of the large sarcophagi and the place left blank, as if the scribe had not had

time to fill in that of the new occupant, but we may probably find the names of those later occupants on their inner mummy cases. One of the largest of these sarcophagi is surcharged with the name of the high priest of Amen, Pinotem.

As soon as we have cleared the lower vault I shall attack the upper chamber or chambers.[3]

In the end, crowded in the tomb were thirty-two baskets (fifteen containing food, six with floral garlands), one wooden bed, six wooden boxes (five containing pottery, one containing detached wooden beards and hands from coffins), sixteen canopic jars, five pairs of sandals, two fans, 110 *shabti* boxes, seventy-nine wood statues (seventy-seven

BRINGING OUT THE MUMMIES.

FIGURES 22, 23 (*opposite top*), 24 (*opposite bottom*).
The discovery of the Bab el-Gasus cache. The hurried clearance, inventory, and transport of the cache thrilled visitors and were widely reported in the international press. From J. Lynch, *Egyptian Sketches* (London, 1890), p. 601, and *The Illustrated London News*, February 28, 1891, p. 268.

Ptah-Sokar-Osiris figures, most containing a papyrus), a pair of mourning figures of the goddesses Isis and Nephthys, and eight wooden stelae, along with 101 sets of inner and outer coffins and 52 single coffins, making a total of 254 coffins (figures 22–24).[4]

There was a great deal of confusion in recording the contents of the cache, and many of the nested sets of coffins had been dismantled by the excavators to make them easier to remove from the tomb. Some of the inner coffins were separated from their outer cases, and it appears that some may have been mismatched from the beginning, when they were first placed in the tomb in antiquity. Adding more mystery, the names of the original owners had been erased on some coffins. Further muddling the situation, excavators and later officials in the Cairo Museum applied several numbering systems to the coffins that were not consistent and did not always agree. Faced with the enormous number of antiquities from this, the largest intact tomb ever found in Egypt, the Egyptian government decided to present some of the coffins as diplomatic gifts and

DISCOVERIES AT THEBES, UPPER EGYPT: BRINGING THE MUMMIES FROM THE RAMESEUM.

sell off the remainder deemed not needed by the Cairo Museum.[5]

Samuel Brown purchased a mummy and the bottom of a coffin for the Albany Institute of History & Art from this surplus,[6] while the attractive lid and coffin board (or mummy cover) had been sold off separately and are now in the British Museum. The ensemble belonged to a man named Ankhefenmut; like the owners of the other coffins in the cache, he belonged to the class of priests and officials of the Temple of Amun at Karnak, the greatest of all of Egypt's religious centers.

DISCOVERIES AT THEBES, UPPER EGYPT: THE FIRST MUMMIES FROM THE RECENT EXCAVATIONS.

The name Ankhefenmut[7] (figure 25) translates as "He lives for the goddess Mut." It is not a coincidence that Ankhefenmut also holds titles indicating that he served Mut, since personal names in ancient Egypt often included the name of a deity. In this way, every time the name was spoken, the god was invoked and thereby an individual was continuously protected by his or her deity. Priests were known to change their own names to include a name compounded with that of a god when they entered the temple service of that deity. The names they selected for their children also reflected the god they served.[8] Their names and their titles were commonly passed on to their offspring.

Searching for Albany's Ankhefenmut in the ancient record is challenging. Neither of his parents is named on any of the parts of the coffin ensemble. If they were, it would have provided more leads and a greater chance to pinpoint who he was. Although there are a number of individuals that date to the same time period who have the same name, not one has the exact same titles. It has also not been possible to locate any family connections on the coffin board in the British Museum that belongs with this coffin.[9] Thus there are a number of individuals named Ankhefenmut, though none can be positively identified with the Albany coffin.

The titles recorded on Ankhefenmut's coffin were *wab*-priest and sculptor of the temple of the goddess Mut.

The Mut Temple
Mut was the consort of Amun-Re, and her cult-temple was at Thebes, its ruins lying to the south of the great Temple of Amun-Re at Karnak (figure 26).

Most Egyptian gods were conceived as belonging to family groups, and Mut was identified as the wife of Amun-Re (figure 27) in the Theban Triad, which also included their son, the moon god Khonsu. *Mut* was

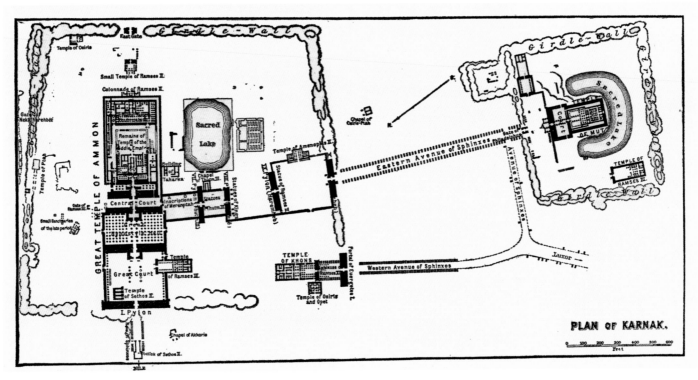

FIGURE 27. Stela fragment with Mut and Amun. New Kingdom, 18th Dynasty, ca. 1550–1295 BC. Limestone. AIHA, gift in honor of the Albany Institute's 225th birthday, 2016.12. This fragment of a small, round-topped votive stela depicts the god Amun with his tall, feathered crown and his consort, the goddess Mut, wearing the double crown of Upper and Lower Egypt behind him. The dedicant has drawn two ears on the stela to make sure the gods hear his prayers.

also the word for "mother" in ancient Egyptian and was written with the hieroglyph of a vulture. She had a number of epithets, including Eye of Re, Queen of the Goddesses, Lady of Heaven, Mother of the Gods, and She Who Gives Birth, But Was Herself Not Born of Any.

Mut was usually depicted as a woman wearing the double crown of Upper and Lower Egypt (figure 28), but she could also be shown with vulture wings or as a vulture itself. She was associated with various other female goddesses, including Nut, Hathor, and Isis, as well as the feline goddesses Bastet and Sekhmet.

Mut's principal cult center was just south of the temple of Amun at Karnak in an area known as Isheru (or Asher) for the spring-fed, crescent-shaped lake that encircles the temple proper.[10] The precinct of Mut has several small temples associated with the main temple, which was enlarged and altered many times over a period of more than 1,000 years. The temple was also furnished with a wealth of sculpture, including dozens of black granite statues of the lion-headed goddess Sekhmet (figures 29–30) that had been relocated to the courtyard of the Mut temple from the mortuary temple of Amenhotep III on the opposite side of the river. In addition to those, many other images of kings and queens, gods and goddesses, and even private people were commissioned to decorate the temple. As a sculptor attached to it, Ankhefenmut would probably have made a number of them.

Wab-Priest

Priests generally performed a critical role in ancient Egyptian temples, since they were responsible for maintaining the cult of the gods housed within the temple (figure 31). The statues of the gods were treated as if they were living and were washed, anointed, dressed, and offered the finest of foods and drink. Priests performed these and countless other daily rituals that were necessary to bring the power of life into the divine image. These rites enabled the gods to maintain the order of the society, the country, and even the universe.

The priesthood of each temple included a small core of permanent priests and a large staff of lay individuals. These upper-class men and women offered their time to the temple in exchange for status, religious protection, and of course the offerings left on the altar that the god did not consume. The elite volunteers served the temple part-time and then returned to their regular jobs.[11] They were involved in temple maintenance and religious ceremonies. The particular tasks they were able to perform depended on the level of priestly ranking they had attained.[12]

Ankhefenmut served as a *wab*,[13] an entry-level priest who would have played a minor role in the sacred temple rituals. The term *wab* means "to purify," and the *wab* is called the "Pure Priest." They were relegated to the rituals that took place in the outer court or outside of the temple. Some texts describe some of the specific tasks that a *wab* performed in the outer court: lighting a lamp, getting the incense burner, placing the coal on the incense burner, placing the incense on the fire, and carrying the situla, a pail filled with holy water or other liquid offerings (figure 32).[14]

The temple became holier as one moved into the interior, closer to where the statue of the god was housed. The *wab*-priests could not participate in the rituals that took place in

FIGURE 28. Statuette of the goddess Mut. Third Intermediate Period, ca. 1069–664 BC. Bronze. AIHA, gift of Heinrich Medicus, 2013.1.7. The name of the goddess Mut means "mother" in ancient Egyptian, and she was revered as the "mother of the world" as well as the consort of the chief state god, Amun. She was also associated with kingship and is depicted wearing the royal double crown.

SEKHET STATUES NEAR THE TEMPLE OF MUT, KARNAK.

the inner rooms of the temple. Most important, they could not see the god's image kept in the shrine. Only the higher-ranking priests could enter the presence of the god. The *wab* had to go through additional initiations to elevate his rank to a higher priestly level.

As a *wab*-priest in the temple, Ankhefenmut would have taken part in a number of ceremonies and devotionals. One of the more socially prestigious duties of the *wab* was to carry the sacred boat. This was the boat that held the shrine containing the statue of the god, and it was transported whenever the image of the god had to travel outside the temple, for example, to another temple during special festivals or ceremonies (figure 33). For these events, the local community gathered to watch as it passed by. As it was carried outside the temple, it was available to issue an oracle, where members of the community could ask the god to pass judgment on a question. The crowds would gather to hear the verdict. In the illustrated Brooklyn Oracle Papyrus, the *wab*-priests are shown carrying the barque for one such oracle.[15] The *wab*-priests holding the barque controlled the movement of the boat and were responsible for revealing the will of the god. The priests would all surge forward if the god's answer was "yes," and backward

FIGURE 30. Bust of Sekhmet. New Kingdom, 18th Dynasty, reign of Amenhotep III, ca. 1390–1352 BC. Gabbro. Temple of Mut at Karnak. Phoebe A. Hearst Museum of Anthropology, 5-365. Photograph courtesy of the Phoebe A. Hearst Museum. The goddess Sekhmet was called upon to punish humankind, who had shown the god Re disrespect. But so blood-thirsty was she that she threatened to destroy all humanity, so the gods deceived her by putting red ochre in the Nile to turn the water blood red, and by making her so drunk that she was convinced of the success of her slaughter. Thereafter, an annual feast held at the temple of Mut that included much drinking became an extremely popular event to celebrate humanity's deliverance.

for a "no." No doubt Ankhefenmut would have presided over activities such as these. Even though the *wab* held a lower rank, being included in the priestly class at all was a great privilege and status symbol. It is certain that Ankhefenmut held an elevated social rank in his society.

Many of the priestly positions were passed on from parent to child. Ankhefenmut likely inherited his title from his father, or he was selected because his family had connections to the temple. A priest named Nebnetcherew in the 22nd Dynasty claimed, "I saw my sons as great priests, son after son who issued from me."[16]

Sculptor in the Temple of Mut

Unlike the full-time priests of the temple, *wab*-priests could hold other jobs, such as "overseers of painters and designers, artisan chiefs of the sacred domain or simple artisans themselves."[17] It is in keeping with what is known of his position that Ankhefenmut could be both a *wab* and a sculptor in the temple. This is demonstrated by the inscription of another *wab*-priest who was employed as a carpenter of the temple of Mut: "A boon which the King gives (to) [Re-Horakhty] foremost of the West, that he may give provisions and incense (to) the *wab*-priest and carpenter of the temple of Mut, Iufaa, son of Padimut."[18]

Craftsmen worked in groups and could be assigned to either the temple or royal atelier.[19] Ankhefenmut's title tells us that he was in the temple workshop. The temple complexes contained a variety of installations that produced the goods necessary for running the temple. Besides the obvious bakeries and breweries, there were also workshops to make objects that were needed "to provide and repair objects such as cult images and items of temple furniture used in the service of the gods."[20] This must have been where Ankhefenmut would have worked.[21]

Egyptian statues were roughed out of blocks of stone using mostly stone tools, with expensive bronze implements reserved for the final details. During Ankhefenmut's time, iron was still a rare and valuable metal and not likely to be used for such tools. Depending on its size, the roughed-out sculpture would be finished by one or a number of men and receive a final polish using special rubbing stones and finer and finer grades of sand abrasives. The stone was then painted and sometimes even gilded.

The term for sculptor, *sankh*, literally means "to cause to live,"[22] which describes how sculptors "brought to life" creations from inanimate materials. Although there is not much detailed information about the exact work that was that was done by a *sankh*, some information comes from a New Kingdom tomb scene depicting a sculptor's workshop (figure 34). Here several men sculpting objects are identified as *sankh*.[23] The central image shows the overseer of sculptors, luty-luty, carving a sculpture of

FIGURE 32. Situla. Late Period to Ptolemaic Period, ca. 664–30 BC. Bronze. AIHA, gift of Heinrich Medicus, 2013.1.12. Priests carried holy water and other liquid offerings in a bronze pail called a situla. This was part of the daily ritual of offerings to be performed in the temple. On the sides of this example is shown a priest offering to the god Min and the goddesses Isis, Hatmehit, and Nephthys, along with Osiris, Horus, and Thoth. Above them, the boat of the sun is shown crossing the sky, pulled by jackals and worshiped by baboons. At the bottom are the god Nefertum and two Apis bulls, along with Sobek, Thueris, Hathor, and the Souls of Pe. The bottom of the vessel is shaped like an open lotus flower, and the two loops at the top once held the handle.

the princess Beketaton. One *sankh* stands by the overseer, watching attentively. Four others identified as *sankh* are seated on stools, carving various small objects on stands in front of them: one carves a chair leg and another a small human head.[24]

The title *sankh* is rare, and of the 211 published coffins of the 21st Dynasty, there is not one individual besides Ankhefenmut who has this title.[25] In the vast indexes of *shabtis*, this title is not encountered. Although numerous *shabtis* are inscribed with the

name Ankhefenmut, none record the titles of the Albany Ankhefenmut.[26] There are clay *shabti*s inscribed for Ankhefenmut from the cache at Bab el-Gasus (now in the British Museum), which were acquired with the mummy board (see below) of Ankhefenmut and perhaps belong to him (figure 35). He may have had other positions that are not identified on his coffin. His finely decorated and elaborate coffin ensemble suggests that he was an important person and may have held more titles that have not yet been discovered.

ANKHEFENMUT'S LIFE AS A PRIEST

FIGURE 33. Aegis of the goddess Isis. Late Period, ca. 664–332 BC. Bronze. AIHA, gift of Heinrich Medicus, 2013.1.11. An image of the head of a god or goddess wearing an exaggerated broad collar, called an aegis, could be used as a figurehead on the prow of a sacred boat or carried as a standard atop a long pole. This image shows a goddess wearing a modius, a small cap decorated with cobras, and cow horns with a sun disk between them. This could represent a number of goddesses, including Isis and Hathor.

Ankhefenmut may have lived within the temple complex or in the surrounding city of Thebes (or Waset, as it was then known). Excavators discovered some houses within the complex[27] built of unbaked mud brick, as most Egyptian domestic construction was, and these dwellings are thought to have housed some of the priests and staff of the temple. Within Karnak's vast grounds were orchards, gardens, wells, workshops, bakeries, breweries, and storerooms. In return for his service at the temple, Ankhefenmut would have been given a share of this abundance. The staples of the ancient Egyptian diet were bread and beer. Bread was baked in heated pottery molds; this low-temperature cooking allowed the yeast to survive so that some of it could be soaked in water, left to ferment, and made into beer. Vegetables and fruit were also available in the temple, including pomegranates, figs, grapes, melon, onions, and lettuce, along with nuts from the dom palm. Meat in the form of beef, lamb, and pork was a rare treat, as were duck and goose. Eggs, honey, milk, and water also made up part of the diet.

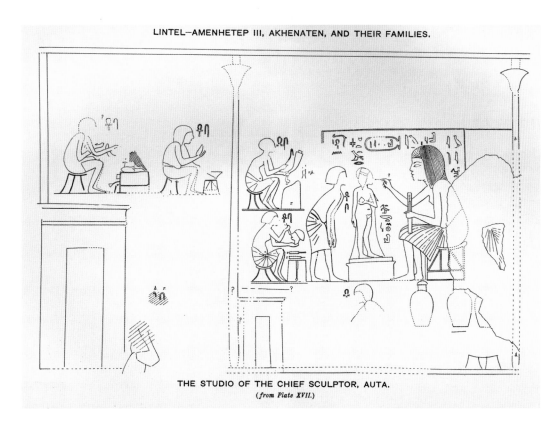

LINTEL—AMENHETEP III, AKHENATEN, AND THEIR FAMILIES.

THE STUDIO OF THE CHIEF SCULPTOR, AUTA.
(from Plate XVII.)

FIGURE 34. Scene from the tomb of Huy at Amarna showing sculptors at work. From N. de G. Davies, *The Rock Tombs of El Amarna* (London, 1905), plate 18.

FIGURE 35. *Shabti* of Ankhefenmut. Third Intermediate Period, 21st Dynasty, ca. 1069–945 BC. Ceramic. British Museum, donated by the Government of the British Protectorate of Egypt, EA24807. Photograph courtesy of the Trustees of the British Museum. This is one of the two clay *shabti* figures given to the British Museum along with Ankhefenmut's coffin board. These appear to be the only ones known for him.

Wine was drunk by the upper classes and was "estate bottled" in vineyards belonging to the king and the temples.

Vast quantities of linen were offered to the temple, and Ankhefenmut is shown on his coffin wearing the flowing, pleated robes that were in fashion during the Ramesside and Third Intermediate Periods.[28] A long linen garment was found in the coffin with the mummy. It had long sleeves, a fringed hem, and a simple V-neck (figure 36).[29] Other types of priests wore additional elements of costume, including a leopard skin for the *sem* or funerary priest, a sash for the lector priest, a scapular for acolytes of Montu, and a sidelock of hair for the clergy of Ptah.[30]

Most linen was plain white; for a touch of color, men and women relied on jewelry

Ankhefenmut and His World   45

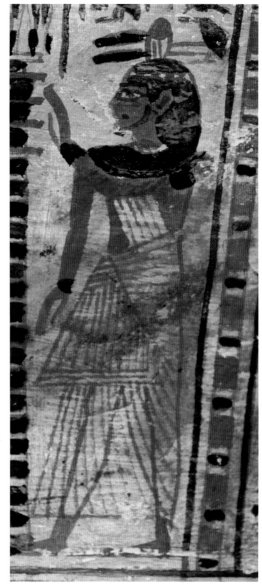

FIGURE 36. Priest's cassock, Thomas Nelson, 2013. Oil on prepared matte board. Private collection. The linen garment found with Ankhefenmut's mummy was undoubtedly a priest's cassock or tunic, such as the one reconstructed in this image. These long vestments would have been worn over a fine linen kilt, under a pleated linen robe.

FIGURE 37. Head of a man. New Kingdom, 18th Dynasty, ca. 1550–1295 BC. Granite. AIHA, gift of Heinrich Medicus, 2013.1.5. Although priests had to be shaven-headed for their work in the temple, they may have worn wigs in other aspects of their lives. This bust of a man shows him with an elaborately curled wig such as what may have been worn by Ankhefenmut.

FIGURE 38. Detail from the coffin base of Ankhefenmut. Third Intermediate Period, 21st Dynasty, ca. 1069–945 BC. Wood, gesso, and pigment. Bab el-Gasus. AIHA, gift of Samuel W. Brown, 1909.18.1b. Ankhefenmut is depicted on his coffin wearing an elaborate robe and a cone of scented fat on his head.

made of semi-precious stones or polychrome faience. Scarabs, signifying rebirth, along with a variety of other amulets were worn by both the living and the dead. A standard item of adornment, the broad collar was worn by both sexes and imitated floral collars, which also symbolized resurrection. Broad collars were composed of rows of faience beads hung from terminals at the shoulders, with a counterweight at the back, known as a *menat*, to keep them from slipping forward. These *menat*s eventually became items of adornment of themselves and were associated with the cult of Hathor. Simple strings of beads could be worn as necklaces, bracelets, or fillets around the head. Priests could also wear images or symbols of their patron god.

Priests were required to be shaven, and Ankhefenmut is shown on his coffin with both a shaven head and long hair, possibly a wig. Egyptians wore elaborately curled wigs (figure 37) made of human hair and beeswax. A cone of scented fat is often shown on the head; it acted as an all-day deodorant as it slowly melted and exuded fragrance (figure 38). Men and women used cosmetics, oils, and lotions to keep their skin from drying in the hot sun and black kohl around the eyes to fight the glare. On their feet, priests wore sandals woven of palm fiber and papyrus, which were a mark of status, as was a wooden walking stick or staff, carried as a sign of authority.

Gifts from royal estates and the general populace, as well as offerings from foreign conquests, flowed into the temples, making them wealthy beyond measure. Priests could sell images of the gods or mummies of their mascot animals to pilgrims visiting temples and sacred sites.

LIFE IN THE 21ST DYNASTY

The 21st Dynasty was the beginning of what is called the Third Intermediate Period, an era of rival dynasties and economic decline in Egypt. The great wealth amassed by the temples made them very powerful, and none more so than Karnak (figures 39 and 40). The 21st Dynasty saw a struggle for the throne between the kings ruling in the Delta city of Tanis and the high priests of the Temple of Amun at Karnak. Ramesses XI, the last pharaoh of the New Kingdom, died without a male heir, and Smendes of Tanis and Pinedjem I, the high priest of Amun at Karnak, married Ramesses's daughters to try to cement their claims to the throne. There does not seem to have been open civil war, but more a jockeying for power and prestige. Although Pinedjem used royal titles and wrote his name in a cartouche, his authority did not appear to extend to all of Egypt; Smendes is attested as king on a few monuments from Upper Egypt. The kings at Tanis tried to create a "northern Karnak" in the Delta, and the temple there was modeled on the complex at Thebes. The rival rulers seem to have negotiated a truce through family ties and continued to intermarry.

This period was one of instability throughout the ancient world and followed the Bronze Age collapse in the Near East. Many of the

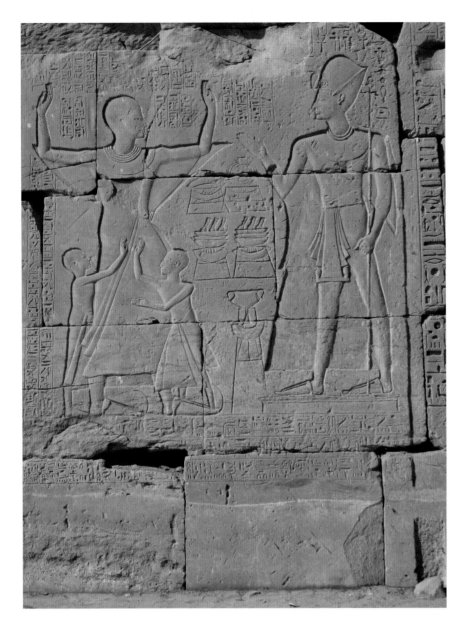

been recycled from the tombs they opened in the Valley of the Kings under the guise of protecting the royal mummies.[31] The bodies and coffins of the kings and queens of the New Kingdom were relocated to a mass burial in a tunnel-like tomb like the Bab el-Gasus. This one was cut into the cliffs high above Deir el-Bahri, and in it were placed royal mummies, the mummies and coffins of high priests of Amun, and their families. This secret cache was later discovered by tomb robbers sometime in the late nineteenth century. Eventually, when the authorities in Cairo became aware of the importance of the find, they sent investigators to discover its whereabouts. The location of the secret tomb was revealed, and its remaining contents, including more than fifty mummies of kings, queens, and high officials, were sequestered and brought to the museum in Cairo in 1881.[32]

great empires had been destroyed by marauding pirates known as the "sea peoples," who had even staged raids on Egypt.

This strife undoubtedly further weakened the economy of Egypt, and that was manifested in the funerary art of the period. The kings in the Delta had far smaller tombs than their predecessors did, and much of their funerary equipment appears to have

It appears that during the Third Intermediate Period many New Kingdom private tombs in Thebes were opened and their contents reused. Many of the coffins from the priests' cache seem to have been earlier 18th and 19th Dynasty anthropoid coffins that were stripped down to recycle the scarce and valuable wood and redecorated to fit the current taste.[33]

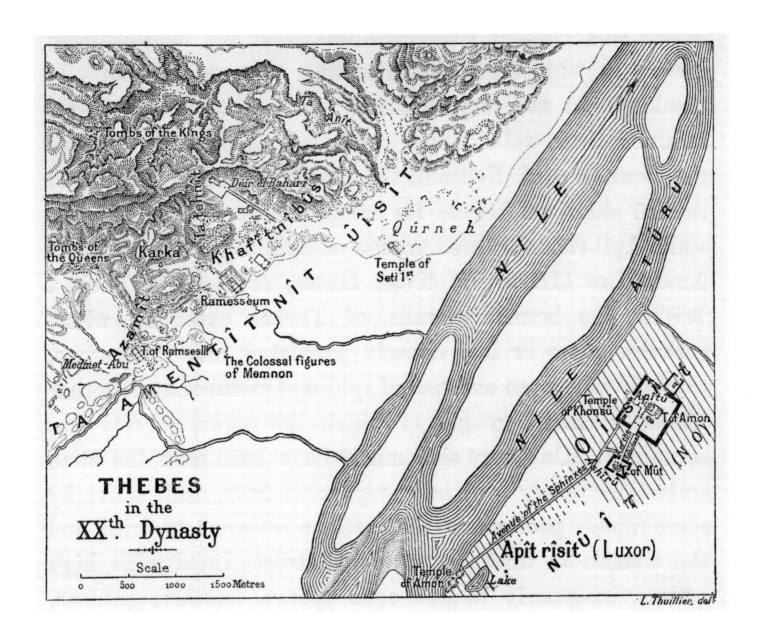

THE DEATH OF ANKHEFENMUT

FIGURE 40. Map of Thebes in the 20th Dynasty. The great temples of Karnak and Luxor were situated on the eastern bank of the Nile at Thebes, while the tombs and temples dedicated to the deceased kings were located on the west bank. From J. H. Breasted, *A History of Egypt* (New York, 1909).

Amid the impoverishment of the Third Intermediate Period, people could no longer afford their own decorated tomb stocked with possessions or a coffin made of fine timber. Ankhefenmut was fortunate; because he was a priest, he was able to obtain a coffin from one of the temple workshops. These coffins seem to have been premade and uninscribed, waiting to be customized for the eventual occupant. Even canopic jars, which in earlier times held viscera removed during mummification, were largely dispensed with, and once the internal organs were removed, they were individually desiccated, wrapped, and returned to the body cavity, sometimes accompanied by small

FIGURE 41. Set of canopic jars. Late Period, 26th Dynasty, ca. 664–525 BC. Limestone. The Metropolitan Museum of Art, gift of Miss Helen Miller Gould, 10.130.1002 (a–d). The lids on these jars represent the Four Sons of Horus: the baboon-headed Hapi, guardian of the lungs; the jackal-headed Dua-mutef, protector of the stomach; the human-headed Imsety, who watched over the liver; and the falcon-headed Qebehsenuef, who protected the intestines. The "dummy" jars were made with no internal space to hold the organs.

wax figures of the Four Sons of Horus. Canopic jars were included in some burials of the period, but because they were no longer used to hold the internal organs, they were slapdash creations that had no internal space and sometimes did not even open. Each carved lid represented one of the Four Sons of Horus (figure 41).

Once the internal organs had been removed, natron, a naturally occurring salt that is mostly a combination of sodium chloride and bicarbonate of soda, was the chief ingredient in drying and preserving the mummy (see "The Mummification of Ankhefenmut," p. 89.). The mummy was dried by packing it in the salt; linen bags of natron were used to stuff the internal body cavity of the mummy. Natron also was used as a cleansing agent and signified purity (figure 42).

The incision made by the embalmers, ideally with a sharp obsidian knife, to remove the internal organs and later pack the body cavity, was sealed with a plate of wax, cartonnage, or metal and embellished with the Eye of Horus to magically heal the body. Tree resins poured over the mummy and coffin darkened and hardened and were mistaken for bitumen, which was called in Arabic *mummiya*, which led to the term "mummy." The mummy was then adorned with amulets to protect the various parts of the body: a headrest amulet to safeguard the head, a *djed*-pillar for the spine, a *sa*-sign for well-being, a heart amulet to protect the heart, and a heart scarab inscribed with a spell to prevent self-incrimination when the heart was weighed against the feather of truth in the final judgment. There were images of the funerary gods: Four Sons of Horus; Isis, Osiris, and Nephthys; and Thoth and Anubis. Images of scarabs and winged scarabs to invoke resurrection were included as amulets or woven into bead nets placed over the

body. Sometimes old garments were used to cover the wrapped body, along with specially woven shrouds. The body itself was wrapped in yards of linen. Ankhefenmut was bandaged in the typical style of the period, with alternating bands of uninscribed linen strips arranged vertically and then horizontally over the body and crisscrossed over the chest.

Because more than one person was mummified in the embalmer's workshop simultaneously, individuals were identified with wooden tags known as "mummy labels." These served the immediate practical function of identifying the deceased and the long-term goal of recording the name for eternity. The Egyptians believed that preserving the name of the deceased was just as important as preserving the body.

Small stelae were sometimes set up outside the rough mud-brick vaulted tombs found from this period. They depicted the deceased worshipping a god, asking that he provide food and other offerings for the tomb owner. Rather than using more costly stone, the craftsmen simply painted scenes and inscriptions onto a wooden board intended to look like a carved stone stela (figure 43).

For his funeral, Ankhefenmut's body would have been transported by boat across

FIGURE 42. These scenes from a coffin now in the Roemer-und Pelizaeus-Museum in Hildesheim are the most complete ancient record we have of the mummification process, showing the body being washed and anointed (below), placed on an embalming table (middle) and wrapped (top). Drawing courtesy of Yvonne Markowitz.

FIGURE 43. Fragment of a stela. Third Intermediate Period, 21st Dynasty, ca. 1069–945 BC. Wood and pigment. AIHA, gift of Dr. Peter Lacovara in honor of Erika Sanger, 2008.15.1. During the Third Intermediate Period, as a shortcut to making carved stone stelae, tombstone-shaped wooden boards were decorated to make them look like painted stone stelae.

the Nile to the west, the land of the dead, to eventually be interred in the Bab el-Gasus mass grave. The coffins found in this cache may have been relocated from other tombs to this large deposit in front of the Deir

FIGURE 44. Painted votive cloth. New Kingdom, late 18th Dynasty to early 19th Dynasty, ca. 1300–1200 BC. Lent by the Dubroff Family Trust. Photograph courtesy of the Metropolitan Museum of Art. Textiles like this were left as gifts to the goddess Hathor at the temple at Deir el-Bahri. The goddess is depicted here in the form of a cow in a boat within a papyrus thicket. A family group standing before Hathor is led by the figure of the priest Tja-nefer, who stands with his arms raised in adoration. The inscription above the figures names the priest and his family and asks the goddess for "life, prosperity, health, alertness(?), praise/favor, and love." Similar scenes of Hathor, the goddess of the Deir el-Bahri area, can be found on many of the coffins of the 21st Dynasty, including that of Ankhefenmut.

el-Bahri temple at some point in the middle of the 21st Dynasty, during the reign of King Amenemope (ca. 993–984 BC). The temple, which had been built nearly 500 years before, during the reign of Hatshepsut, had become the focus of a funerary cult associated with the goddess Hathor and the annual festival of Osiris known as "the beautiful feast of the Valley." The temple's causeway was used for funeral and festival processions, and people would make offerings at the tombs of their ancestors or leave gifts to the goddess Hathor of Deir el-Bahri, including shrouds painted with the image of the cow-goddess emerging from a tomb in the desert (figure 44).

THE COFFIN OF ANKHEFENMUT

Despite being a time of impoverishment, in many ways the Third Intermediate Period was the zenith of coffin decoration. The magical texts of the Book of the Dead (see below) were commonly written on the walls in New Kingdom tombs, but by the 21st Dynasty the political and economic deterioration, as well as rampant tomb robbery, created a movement away from elaborate tombs. Because of this, caves, pits, and older reused tombs became the repositories of the coffins, and the walls of the tombs were no longer available for texts and paintings. Because most people could no longer afford painted tombs and large amounts of ritual grave goods, the coffin itself took on all the symbolic representation necessary to protect the deceased and ensure a safe journey to the next world. The intricate mythological scenes painted in jewel-like colors on these coffins have been likened to the effect of medieval stained-glass windows.[34] The brightly painted decorations are sometimes rendered in gesso to give them a three-dimensional quality. Amulets and vignettes from the Book of the Dead ornament the exterior of these coffins, and they are all coated with a golden yellow varnish. Often underneath the lid was placed a mummy board or coffin board, an outgrowth of earlier mummy masks, which served as another canvas for more magical symbols to protect the body (figure 45).

As far as we can tell, Ankhefenmut appears to have had only a single coffin, not a nested set. The coffin had been roughly constructed of irregular boards made of local softwood. The lid was attached to the base by a series of mortise and tenon joints running along the sides of the coffin. The wood was covered with a mixture of gypsum plaster and mud called gesso, painted with color, and then varnished with the resin of the terebinth tree. White was used as a ground, and a varnish created a golden color in imitation of gilded coffins.

Ankhefenmut is depicted on the coffin lid (figure 46a) wearing the long lappet wig of a divinity and crowned with a fillet, with an elaborate garland collar around his chest and shoulders. His crossed arms are covered with stacked beaded bracelets and a pair of winged scarab pectoral ornaments. The goddess Nut is shown protecting the deceased, with her feathered wings stretched across his chest.

The Inscriptions and Scenes on the Coffin of Ankhefenmut

The coffin (figure 47a–o) is covered with religious formulae derived from the Egyptian Book of the Dead, a compilation of prayers and spells designed to ensure the safe journey of the mummy from this world to the heavenly realm and maintain the eternal spiritual life of the deceased. Divided into

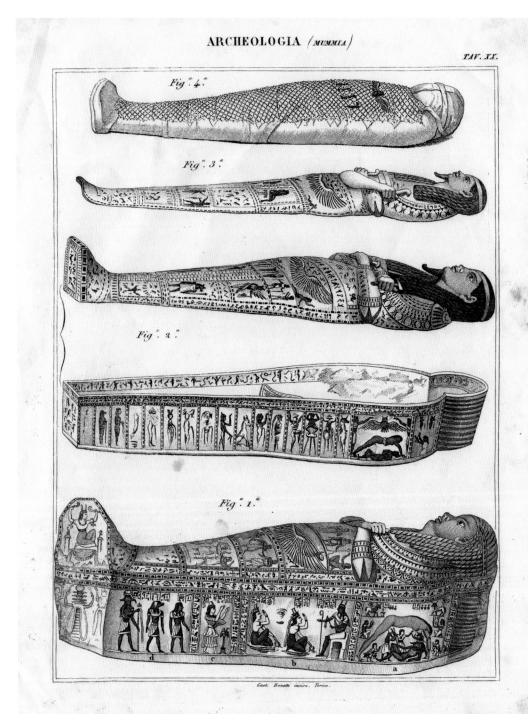

Fig.ª 4.ª

Fig.ª 3.ª

Fig.ª 2.ª

Fig.ª 1.ª

Gaet. Bonatti incise, Torino.

FIGURE 45. A mummy, coffin board, and coffin from the 21st Dynasty. From *Archeologia, Mummia, Nuova Enciclopedia* (1866). Courtesy of Dr. Peter Lacovara. This drawing shows the elements of a typical 21st Dynasty coffin assemblage. They were often made of rough local softwood overlaid with thick layers of mud and gesso, and covered with brightly painted decorations, which included amuletic devices and vignettes from the Book of the Dead. Below the lid was placed a mummy board that served as another canvas for more amuletic symbols to protect the body. The mummy was wrapped and sometimes covered with amulets and a network of faience beads. The coffin set was sometimes nested into an additional mummiform base and lid.

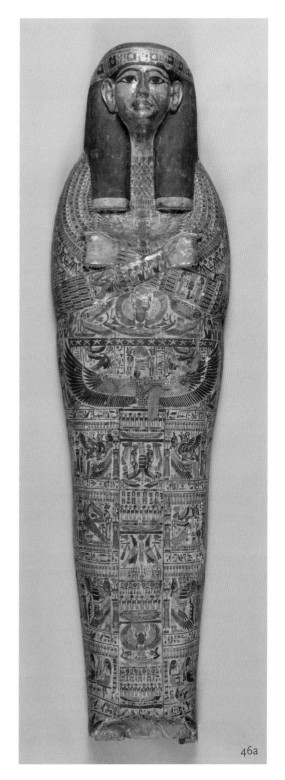

46a

46b

FIGURE 46. (a) Coffin lid of Ankhefenmut. Third Intermediate Period, 21st Dynasty, ca. 1069–945 BC. Wood and pigment. Bab el-Gasus. Kunsthistoriches Museum, Vienna, AE INV 6267a. (b) Mummy board of Ankhefenmut. Third Intermediate Period, 21st Dynasty, ca. 1069–945 BC. Wood and pigment. Bab el-Gasus. British Museum, London, donated by the Government of the British Protectorate of Egypt, EA24797. Photograph courtesy of the Trustees of the British Museum. Ankhefenmut's coffin assemblage included the mummy and the base of the coffin, which are in the Albany Institute of History & Art; the mummy board that was placed over the mummy and under the lid, which is now in the British Museum; and the lid, which is on loan from the Kunsthistoriches Museum in Vienna.

47a

47c

47d

47e

FIGURE 47A, C–H.
Right side:

Coffin base of Ankhefenmut. Third Intermediate Period, 21st Dynasty, ca. 1069–945 BC. Wood, gesso, and pigment. Bab el-Gasus. AIHA, gift of Samuel W. Brown, 1909.18.1b. The sides of the coffin base of Ankhefenmut are decorated with gods and mythological scenes to protect him on his journey to the afterlife. The scene on the head end would have been the image of the goddess Nephthys, but it has been rubbed away, probably when put into or taken out of the tomb. A column of hieroglyphic text beside it reads "Nephthys, sister of a god, eye of Re, mistress of the necropolis in the West."

(c) There are two registers in this scene. The bottom depicts the mummy lying flat on the Earth. Over the mummy are six sun disks representing daylight hours and six stars representing hours of the night. There are also six *nefer*-signs, symbols of all that is good, flanked by two protective *wedjet*-eyes. Above the mummy is the canopy of heaven, symbol of

the sky. The upper register depicts the solar boat containing a scarab beetle pushing the rising sun, a powerful symbol for rebirth.

(d) In this scene, Ankhefenmut is depicted twice, each time offering the *djed*-pillar to Osiris and Sokar-Osiris. On the right, he stands wearing a shoulder-length hairstyle and beard, offering the *djed*-pillar to a seated Osiris, whose name is written above him as "Osiris, lord." Ankhefenmut's name and the title *wab*-priest are written above him. On the left, he offers the *djed*-pillar to Ptah-Sokar, a seated falcon-headed god. Ankhefenmut is shown bald and clean-shaven, a more priestly look.

(e) Here the standing figure of the human-headed Imsety, one of the Four Sons of Horus, who protected the liver, faces left. He holds the scepter in his right hand and the flail and the ankh in his left. His name is written above him in two columns of hieroglyphs.

47f

47g

47h

(f) Nephthys is shown twice in this scene, identified both times by the symbol of her crown, which spells her name. On the left, she is kneeling facing right, with her left hand to her forehead in a typical gesture of mourning. She holds the *shen*, symbol of eternity, in her right hand. The protective *wedjet*-eye of Horus is above. The text written above her head reads: "Nephthys, sister of the god." She kneels before the Abydos standard of Osiris, which is protected by the standing winged goddess Nephthys again.

(g) Hapi, with the head of a baboon, is one of the Four Sons of Horus and the guardian of the lungs. He stands in a shrine facing to the left, holding the scepter, flail, and ankh-sign.

(h) Ankhefenmut kneels before the goddess of the heavens, Nut, who stands within a sycamore tree. She is often shown offering food and water to Ankhefenmut and his *ba*, his soul, represented as a human-headed bird. The dotted lines going from the *ba* to Nut and from Ankhefenmut to Nut represent the goddess giving him the eternal "water of life." She is holding a loaf of bread and a vase of water. Sycamores were often planted near gardens and tombs, where it was believed that Nut comforted the dead, and coffins were frequently made of its wood.

47b

47i

47j

47k

47l

FIGURE 47B, 47I–O.

Left side:

(i) Facing to the right, the falcon crowned with a sun disk represents the sun god. He stands on the symbol for unification of the "two lands" of Upper and Lower Egypt, the *sema-tawy*, which is composed of entwined lotus and papyrus plants. A cobra goddess behind the falcon protectively holds her wings around him. In front of him is a small rearing cobra wearing the white crown of Upper Egypt.

(j) Ankhefenmut stands facing to the left with arms upraised, adoring the seated composite god Ptah-Sokar-Osiris and about to pour an offering from a ritual *nemset* vase. He stands before a small table of offerings. Above him and the falcon-headed god is the word "adoring." Nephthys stands behind Ptah-Sokar-Osiris with her protective outstretched wings around him.

(k) As on the right side of the coffin, Imsety stands here with the scepter and flail.

(l) Another image of Hapi.

47m

47n

47o

(m) The god Duamutef was another one of the Four Sons of Horus. He had the head of a jackal and guarded the deceased's stomach after mummification.

(n) Qebehsenuef is the final of the Four Sons of Horus. He has the head of a hawk and the body of a human, and he protected the intestines.

(o) In this image, a cow, representing the goddess Hathor, emerges from a tomb in the desert. The tomb has a small pyramid on top, and above the doorway is an inscription that reads "Osiris, lord of eternity." Sand dunes with dotted grains of sand are mounded up against it. Hathor was particularly worshiped at Deir el-Bahri, where this coffin comes from, but she is also associated with Mehetweret, the celestial cow. The stars on her hide indicate that she is a sky goddess.

192 chapters and often illustrated with colorful scenes or vignettes, the Book of the Dead was popular from the early New Kingdom through the end of pharaonic history.[35] As mentioned already, because of the lack of wall space in 21st Dynasty tombs, to keep the vital religious information with the deceased, the Book of the Dead spells were written on the coffins themselves.

Every coffin was a unique creation. There were literally hundreds of possible scenes that could adorn a coffin, and the final decoration was the result of combining several elements. Evidence reveals that in many cases, before death the person chose the types of scenes they would like on their own coffin. The quality of the artwork was directly related what the owner could afford—the more expense, the finer the quality of decoration. Another major influence on the appearance of the casket was regional artistic variations and the particular fashion of the day. The end result is that each coffin is distinctive and requires individual interpretation.

Which Gods Are Invoked and for What Purpose

Every deity, symbol, prayer, and spell on the coffin served the purpose of protecting the deceased, ensuring their rebirth after death, and providing for existence in the next world. This is outlined in Spell 15 from the Book of the Dead:[36]

Worship of Osiris, Lord of Eternity, Wennefer.

Horakhty multiple of forms and great of shapes, Ptah-Sokar, Atum of Heliopolis, Lord of the Shetyt-shrine, who enriches Memphis; these are the gods who govern the Netherworld; they protect you when you go to rest in the Lower Sky. Isis embraces you in peace and drives away the adversary from your path. Turn your face to the West that you may illumine the Two Lands with fine gold. Those who were asleep stand up to look at you; they breathe the air, they see your face like the shining of the sun-disc in its horizon, their hearts are at peace because of what you have done, for to you belong eternity and everlasting.

The gods summoned in the texts on Ankhefenmut's coffin are primarily those of two different myths: the creation myth of Heliopolis that included the sun god Re, with whom the deceased travels through the Netherworld on the solar boat; and the resurrection cult of the god Osiris, king of the gods in the next world. Osiris was mummified, buried, and magically reborn into an eternal spiritual life. Here on Ankhefenmut's coffin, he is also called Ptah-Sokar-Osiris or Ptah-Sokar, a later combination of resurrection and creator gods.

The gods from the Heliopolitan family tree (or ennead) of Re included Atum, Shu, Tefnut, Geb, and Nut. According to this creation story, in the beginning there was nothing but a primeval ocean called *nun*. From the water appeared a mound or island, and on it was the god Atum, or Atum-Re, who gave birth to the god of the air, Shu, and Tefnut, the goddess of moisture, who in turn begat Nut, the sky goddess, and Geb, the earth god. Their children, Osiris, Isis, Seth, and Nephthys, were the principal actors in the great resurrection story. Osiris was believed to have been Egypt's first king, but he was murdered by his brother, Seth, who cut the body into pieces and scattered them all over the world. Isis, the wife of Osiris, and her sister, Nephthys, were able to gather up the pieces and reanimate Osiris so that they could have a child, Horus. Horus set out to

avenge his father's death in an epic battle with Seth. In the course of the fighting, Seth poked out Horus's eye, but it magically came to life and became the healing *wedjet*-eye.

In their roles in this great drama, Osiris became the god of the dead, Horus the protector of the king, Seth the god of chaos, and Isis the great mother. Other deities associated with the cult of the dead include the Four Sons of Horus. Additional gods invoked on the funerary equipment and closely associated with resurrection and protection are Hathor, Selket, Djehuty (Thoth), the *benu*-bird, and the celestial cow, Mehetweret.[37]

Arrangement of Texts on the Coffin of Ankhefenmut

There is one horizontal band of text at the top edge of Ankhefenmut's coffin base. It extends around the whole exterior of the coffin, with the exception of the foot area. Ptah-Sokar-Osiris is invoked on both sides of the surround, coupled with the goddess Selket on the right side and Isis on the left.

Around the exterior of the base, fifteen vertical groups of texts alternate with fourteen different scenes. The placement of texts and scenes is not symmetrical from one side to the other. Because symmetry and duality play such a prominent role in Egyptian art, one would think that they would choose the same number of texts and scenes for each side, but in this case they did not.

The scenes (vignettes) and texts relate different spells from the Book of the Dead. The texts are passages from certain spells, and the vignettes are in most cases illustrations of the Book of the Dead chapters, since a scene without any text can also represent a Book of the Dead chapter.[38]

The passages from the Book of the Dead that were selected for a coffin or a papyrus were not a haphazard or random choice.[39] Any compilation of texts from the Book of the Dead served the same purpose, to ensure that the deceased "goes forth by day," meaning that he or she is reborn and attains eternal life. Scenes show the deceased emerging from the tomb and going out into the world.

> As for one who knows this roll on earth, or if it is put in writing on his coffin, he goes forth by day in any form he wishes.[40]

> In order for the deceased "to go forth by day" or to be successfully reborn in the next world, certain key elements had to be included in the group of prayers and spells for the deceased.[41]

Types of Spells

1. *To arrive in the Beyond.* On his coffin, we can see Ankhefenmut arriving in the next world "Beyond," standing before Osiris (figure 47d).

2. *To be justified in the judgment of the dead.* Becoming justified, or pronounced "true of voice" and worthy of going to the next world, is established at the weighing of the heart before Osiris, recorded by the god Djehuty. Though the actual weighing of the heart scene is not pictured on the coffin, it is alluded to by the Recitation by Djehuty. Djehuty is clearly a reference to the final judgment before the gods. In one of the spells from the Book of the Dead, Djehuty is addressed: "The deceased appeals to Djehuty to vindicate him before the tribunals of the gods."

3. *To participate in the daily cycle of the sun god.* The Egyptians wanted to be eternal, like the sun god who traverses the sky and is reborn daily. On the coffin of Ankhefenmut, we can see the sun god traveling the heavens in his sacred boat (figure 47c).

4. *To set up provisions in offering formulae.* To have eternal offerings was a key to maintaining a spiritual afterlife. The coffin is covered in texts, which include offerings for Ankhefenmut.

5. *Protection by the Sons of Horus*. The Four Sons of Horus figure prominently on this coffin, and protection is offered by them, along with all the deities and their emblems on the coffin (figure 47e, g, k–n).

6. *Uniting of* ba *and mummy*. The *ba* is a spiritual form of the deceased, likened to an individual's unique personality. It lives eternally after death and can take on its own form. It is often depicted as a human-headed bird. One of the spells in the Book of the Dead states: "As for one who knows this spell, his corpse shall not perish, and his soul shall not leave his corpse." So uniting the *ba* with the mummy was essential for spiritual afterlife. Ankhefenmut is shown with his *ba* receiving libations from the tree goddess, a form of Hathor (figure 47h).

7. *Mobility of the* ba. The *ba* regaining mobility after death is key for the eternal spiritual life of the deceased. The *ba* of Ankhefenmut is depicted on the coffin, moving freely (figure 47h).

8. *Repelling dangers of the Netherworld*. For the deceased to arrive safely in the next world and continue to have eternal life, the dangers one could encounter had to be repelled. For this purpose one of Djehuty's epithets is "who drives away the enemy of the sun god Re."

These essential aspects of preserving the mummy and ensuring its eternal spiritual afterlife are the function of the coffin's decoration. However, it has been suggested that the motifs on the coffins of this period may reflect real or symbolic ceremonies and events that took place as part of the final burial ritual.[42] The burial procession would visit and make offerings to local shrines; for instance, in figure 47o, the cow emerging from a tomb in the desert would reflect a visit paid to the Hathor chapel at Deir el-Bahri, and the sycamore tree goddess scene (figure 47h) imitates the actual sycamore trees, which were growing in front of the Mentuhotep temple at Deir el-Bahri.[43] Even the judgment scene would have been a reenacted event that was part of the burial ritual. The solar scenes too may have reflected a visit paid to the solar sanctuary on the third terrace of the Hatshepsut temple. The offering scenes on the coffins also may correspond to real or symbolic offerings made to the various local chapels.[44]

It is not always easy to concretely link a motif with a chapter in the Book of the Dead; one image could be related to a number of different spells, and conversely, one spell could have a number of different images associated with it. A further complication is that some scenes are simply difficult to interpret. On this coffin, some of the vignettes appear to be directly related to the adjacent texts, whereas others do not have an obvious connection.[45]

Types of Texts

There are a number of different classes of inscriptions on the coffin, including the standard offering formula (known as the *hetep di nesewt*), spells to be recited, and salutations to the gods.

1. *Hetep di nesewt*. The *hetep di nesewt*, "An offering which the king and other gods give," is a classic offering formula used throughout most of pharaonic history. Its purpose was to ensure that an eternal supply of food, drink, and all necessities of life were provided for the *ka*, the spirit of the deceased that lived on after death with the body in the tomb, while the *ba* was the aspect of the spirit that could fly between heaven and Earth. The *ka* needed food and drink offerings to be sustained eternally. The *ka* is part of the soul along with the *ba*. This formula

can be found only on the horizontal top band of text on the coffin of Ankhefenmut. There is no mention specifically of the *ka* of Ankhefenmut on the coffin base. Instead the offering is given for "the Osiris, Ankhefenmut, true of voice." Both the terms "the Osiris" and "true of voice" indicate that he is deceased.

2. *Djed medew in*. The Book of the Dead spells are often introduced by the words *djed medew in*, translated as "Words to be spoken by" or "Recitation by." On the coffin of Ankhefenmut, this phrase is found twice on the right side; on the left side, six groupings start with these words.

3. *Inedj hr ek*. The right side of the coffin has four spells that start with "Greeting to you . . . god"; there are none of that type on the left side.

Common Arrangement of Texts

Certain scenes are more likely to be found in specific places on a coffin. For instance, on the Albany coffin, the Four Sons of Horus are depicted on a substantial portion of the left side. This is true of the High Priest Masaharta's coffin, which dates to the early 21st Dynasty, and of his wife Tayuheret, both now in the Cairo Museum, which have a very similar decorative style to that of Ankhefenmut.[46] It has been suggested that the repertoire of the royal/elite workshop was available for the artists decorating lesser coffins, and there were many borrowings.[47] This could explain the similarity between Ankhefenmut's coffin and those of the family of the High Priests of Amun. For example, the scene (figure 47o) of the Hathor cow emerging from the desert tomb, and figure 47h, the tree goddess making offerings, are commonly paired on opposite sides of the royal coffins, as they are here. Both scenes are commonly found specifically at the foot end of the coffin,[48] as they are on the Albany coffin.

Head and Foot Ends

The head end of the coffin is traditionally protected by Nephthys and the foot end by Isis. It seems likely that Nephthys would have been pictured on the head end, which is now destroyed. This is further suggested by the fact that to the left of the head end is a text that invokes Nephthys, who can be found on numerous 21st Dynasty coffins at this end.[49] Although we would expect to see Isis on the foot end, the texts near the foot end of the Albany coffin also invoke Nephthys. It would seem that these texts naming Nephthys in

the position usually reserved for Isis are a scribal error, as occasionally happened on coffins. Isis is only mentioned once on the Albany coffin base, on the horizontal band around the top edge. However, the foot end of the coffin is left blank, rather than containing an image of Isis as in earlier periods. Perhaps since these coffins were stood on their foot during the funerary ceremony, it was thought advisable not to decorate it.

Bottom

Barely visible at the bottom of the interior of the coffin is a very badly damaged, large-scale image of a god similar to those found in other coffins of the period. It is difficult to say who it was, since a number of large-scale figures are used in this position, including Osiris (in various forms), the Goddess of the West, the goddess Nut, and others. The background of the figure and interior sides of the coffin are painted a dark red, as is also typical of the interior ground color of the 21st Dynasty coffins—the dark red is perhaps used to cover up earlier decoration from recycled coffins.

Lid

The coffin was a microcosm of the world; its lid symbolized the heavens and the base the earth. The actual events that took place during the burial ritual are depicted on the base, the earthly realm. The decoration on the lid of Ankefenmut's coffin (figures 46a and 48) is executed in red, green, and blue with yellow varnish. The images are finely delineated with great attention to detail, especially in the central register. The face is framed with a striped wig. A large, elaborate pectoral is worn around the neck of the winged ram-headed scarab. The three-dimensional crossed arms are adorned with ornate bracelets and cuffs decorated with images of deities.[50]

Under the crossed arms is a depiction of the sky goddess Nut, and the lower portion of the lid is divided roughly into three vertical bands of carefully rendered decoration. The foot area of the coffin lid is damaged. The central band of decoration contains primarily solar imagery, including a ram-headed scarab rolling a sun disk, winged sun disks, falcon gods with crowns of Upper and Lower Egypt, winged scarabs rolling the sun across the sky, and the solar boat of the sun god Re.

Flanking the central band on either side are four scenes, each divided by narrow bands of text. The first two bands of text give the name and titles of Ankhefenmut. The rest of the lines of text are prayers for adoring the gods and giving them all good and pure things. The gods named here are also mentioned on the coffin base. They include Osiris, lord of eternity, foremost of the westerners; Hapi; Osiris Wennefer; Isis, the great mother of the god; Nephthys, the great mother of the god; Osiris, lord of eternity; Wennefer, lord of the living; Duamutef; Nephthys, the sister of the god; and Selket. Curiously, two of the Four Sons of Horus are not mentioned (Qebehsenuef and Imsety); also not named is Neith, one of four guardian goddesses.

The four registers of scenes are primarily related to Osiris, Ptah, or Ptah-Sokar-Osiris. In two of the four registers, Ankhefenmut presents offerings. The top registers show especially informative images of Ankhefenmut as he would look performing priestly rituals. He wears a pleated long kilt, his head is shaved, and around it is tied a long fillet knotted in the back. He is offering a smoking pot of incense to the seated god identified as Ptah, behind whom Isis appears with outstretched wings in a protective gesture.

The third register shows Nephthys with wings protecting a tall, narrow object that is known as "the Abydos fetish" and is a symbol of Osiris. The fourth register shows the Sons of Horus. The portion of the foot area below this is damaged but probably would have featured the mourning goddesses Isis and Nephthys on either side.

Mummy Board

The colors used on the mummy board (figures 46b and 49) are more limited than what appears on the lid or coffin base. The sole pigments used are red, black, and yellow; white was used only for the eyes and details of the bead net covering the lower body of the figure. Ankhefenmut is shown wearing the long lappet wig of a divine being, a floral fillet around the top of his head, and a garland collar around his neck and upper body. His arms are crossed, and he wears beaded bracelets along with ones made of amuletic *wedjet*-eyes. On the lower half of the body is a crosshatched design, which imitates a bead net on a red background. The design echoes real nets, made of faience beads, which have been found placed over the mummy inside the coffin in some cases. The vertical and horizontal bands on the lower body match the bandages on the outside of mummies of this period.

A central text on the mummy board of Ankhefenmut includes prayers to Nut, who spanned the heavens, swallowed the sun at evening, and gave birth to it at dawn. Nut is shown on the mummy board kneeling with outstretched wings, protecting and symbolically giving the deceased new life each day, as she does for the sun. Numerous other sun-god images are central on the lid and coffin board: the ram-headed scarab, the scarab beetle rolling the sun, and the scarab in the solar boat traversing the heavens. All images symbolize the daily cycle of the sun and the symbolic rebirth of the sun and the deceased.

The plethora of decorative motifs, scenes, and texts on the coffin were all to ensure Ankhefenmut's transition to eternal life and preserve his memory forever.

NOTES

1. J. Lipinska, "Bab el Gusus: Cache Tomb of the Priests and Priestesses of Amen," *Kmt*, 4, no. 4 (Winter 1993–94), 48–59; A. Niwiński, "The Bab el-Gusus Tomb and the Royal Cache in Deir el-Bahri," *Journal of Egyptian Archaeology*, 70 (1984), 73–81.

2. G. Daressy, "Les sépultures des prêtres d'Ammon à Deir el-Bahari," *Annales du service des antiquités de l'Egypte*, 1 (1900), 141–48.

3. "The Great Discovery of Mummies at Thebes," *Nelson Evening Mail*, vol. 25, no. 182 (August 3, 1891), 4.

FIGURE 48. Coffin lid of
Ankhefenmut. The lid would
have been secured to the base
with wooden tenons and pegs.
On the lid, Ankhefenmut is
shown with the long lappet
wig of a god, and his arms are
crossed in the pose of Osiris.

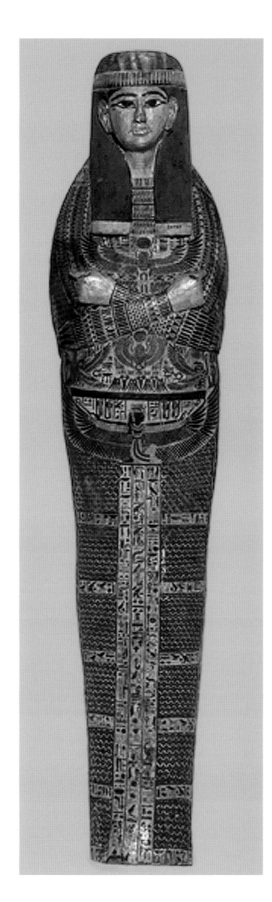

FIGURE 49. Mummy board of Ankhefenmut. The mummy board, or coffin board, was placed over the mummy and under the lid to protect the body and serve as another canvas for protective spells and images. On it, Ankhefenmut is shown wearing the bead-net garment worn by divine beings.

4. N. Reeves, *Ancient Egypt: The Great Discoveries: A Year-by-Year Chronicle* (New York, 2000), 82.

5. Reeves, *Ancient Egypt*, 81–82.

6. AIHA, 1909.18.1a.

7. H. Ranke, *Personennamen*, vol. 1 (Gluckstadt, 1937), 67.8.

8. J. Assmann, *Das kulturelle Gedächtnis: Schrift, Erinnerung und politische Identität in frühen Hochkulturen* (Munich, 1992); J. Assmann, *Ägyptische Geheimnisse* (Munich, 2004), esp. 135ff, 150; H. Jaquet-Gordon, *The Graffiti on the Khonsu Temple Roof at Karnak: A Manifestation of Personal Piety*, Oriental Institute Publications vol. 123 (Chicago, 2003); J. M. Kruchten, *Les annales des prêtres de Karnak (XXIe–XXIIIe dynasties) et autres textes contemporains relatifs à l'initiation des prêtres d'Amon*, Orientalia Lovaniensia Analecta 32 (Leuven, 1989); J. F. Quack, "Königsweihe, Priesterweihe, Isisweihe," in *Ägyptische Mysterien?*, ed. J. Assmann and M. Bommas (Munich, 2002), 95–108.

9. John Taylor, personal correspondence, March 2013.

10. M. Benson, J. A. Gourlay, and P. E. Newberry, *The Temple of Mut in Asher: An Account of the Excavation of the Temple and of the Religious Representations and Objects Found Therein, as Illustrating the History of Egypt and the Main Religious Ideas of the Egyptians* (London, 1899).

11. E. Teeter, *Religion and Ritual in Ancient Egypt* (Cambridge, 2011), 35. "For much of Egyptian history, there was no class of full-time professional priests." Many of the priests were classified as lay priests. This appointment was part-time, and the priest would hold another job, often a position in the state or local governments. The lay priests were especially common in small communities, and they served on a rotation system. Normally, there were four equally staffed groups of lay priests. Each group served for a month and then returned to their other occupation for three months (D. B. Redford, *The Ancient Gods Speak: A Guide to Egyptian Religion* [Oxford, 2002], 315).

12. For the Karnak versions of texts concerning priestly duties, one for the temple of Amonrasonter (P. Berlin 3055) and one for the temple of Mut (P. Berlin 3014+3053), see *Rituale für den Kultus des Amon und für den Kultus der Mut*, in the series Hieratische Papyrus aus den Königlichen Museen zu Berlin (Leipzig, 1901), vol. 1; A. Moret, *Le rituel du culte divin journalier en Égypte, d'après les papyrus de Berlin et les textes du temple de Séti Ier, à Abydos* (Paris, 1902); E. Kausen, "Das tägliche Tempelritual," in *Rituale und Beschwörungen II, Texte aus der Umwelt des Alten Testaments*, Band II: *Religiöse Texte*, Lieferung 3 (Gütersloh, 1988), 391–405.

13. There is also the title *wabet* for female *wab*-priests.

14. J. Gee, "Prophets, Initiation and the Egyptian Temple," *Journal for the Society of the Study of Egyptian Antiquities* 31 (2004), 97.

15. Brooklyn Oracle Papyrus, 26th Dynasty, Brooklyn Museum Acc. No. 47.218.3a–j.

16. Teeter, *Religion and Ritual*, 29, n42.

17. S. Sauneron, *The Priests of Ancient Egypt* (New York, 1980), 70.

18. 18th Dynasty, Fitzwilliam Museum, E.G.A.119.1949.

19. R. H. Wilkinson, *The Complete Temples of Ancient Egypt* (New York, 2000), 75.

20. Wilkinson, *Complete Temples*, 92.

21. One wonders what nonreligious titles were held by Ankhefenmut, because how could a craftsman be paid enough to afford such an elaborate coffin ensemble? However, craftsmen often bartered their skills and crafts with each other.

22. A. Erman and H. Grapow, *Wörterbuch der Aegyptischen Sprache* (Leipzig, 1928), IV 47.17. 23. These scenes come from the tomb of Huya, a steward of Queen Tiye at Amarna. See G. Robins, *The Art of Ancient Egypt* (London, 1997), figure 22; see also figure 21, another New Kingdom workshop scene from the tomb of Rekhmire. Old Kingdom scenes of sculptors at work can be seen in figures 17 (tomb of Ti, 6th Dynasty) and 20 (tomb of Meresankh III, Fourth Dynasty).

24. Other objects are not clear and cannot be identified, as the relief has deteriorated.

25. A. Niwiński, *21st Dynasty Coffins from Thebes: Chronological and Typological Studies* (Mainz am Rhein, 1988), Appendix 2.

26. W. M. F. Petrie, *Shabtis* (London, 1935), xvi; H. Schneider, *Shabtis: An Introduction to the History of Ancient Egyptian Funerary Statuettes* (Leiden, 1977), 4.5.1.1 and 1.2; Rocznik Museum (*Rocznik Museum Narodowego W Warszawie* XI [Warsaw, 1967], 34, no. 31);P. Newberry, *Funerary Statuettes and Model Sarcophagi*, Catalogue général des antiquités égyptiennes du Musée du Caire (Cairo, 1937, plates, 1957), no. 48477.

27. P. Anus and R. Sa'ad, "Habitations de prêtres dans le temple d'Amon de Karnak," *Kêmi: Revue de philology et d'archéologie égyptiennes et coptes*, 21 (1971), 217–38.

28. M. Houston and F. Hornblower, *Ancient Egyptian Costume* (Cairo, 1989), 16–20.

29. AIHA, 1909.18.3; see sidebar, "Ankhefenmut's Tunic."

30. S. Sauneron, *The Priests of Ancient Egypt* (New York, 1980), 40–43.

31. C. Hope, *Gold of the Pharaohs* (Victoria, 1988), 19.

32. E. Graefe and G. Belova, eds., *The Royal Cache TT 320: A Re-Examination* (Cairo, 2010).

33. K. Cooney, "Coffin Reuse in the 21st Dynasty: How and Why Did the Egyptians Reuse the Body Containers of their Ancestors?," *Backdirt: Annual Review of the Cotsen Institute of Archaeology* (2012), 22–33.

34. H. E. Winlock, *Excavations at Deir el Baḥri, 1911–1931* (London, 2001), 109.

35. J. H. Taylor, *Journey through the Afterlife: Ancient Egyptian Book of the Dead* (Cambridge, MA, 2010).

36. R. O. Faulkner, *The Ancient Egyptian Book of the Dead* (Austin, 1999), 40–43.

37. C. Traunecker, *The Gods of Ancient Egypt* (Ithaca, 2001).

38. A. Niwiński, *Studies on the Illustrated Theban Funerary Papyri of the 11th and 10th Centuries B.C.* (Freiburg, 1989), 129.

39. W. Forman and S. Quirke, *Hieroglyphs and the Afterlife in Ancient Egypt* (London, 1996), 145. The time around late 21st Dynasty is when "the variety of the papyri, and of decoration on the ornate wooden coffins, reaches its peak."

40. T. G. Allen, ed., *The Egyptian Book of the Dead* (Chicago, 1974), 65.

41. B. Backes, "Three Funerary Papyri from Thebes: New Evidence on Scribal and Funerary Practice in the Late Period," *British Museum Studies in Ancient Egypt and Sudan* 15 (2010), 1–21. "Indeed, the choice was not made without purpose. By examining the content of the texts and the vignettes it is apparent that they comprise most of what might be called the 'basic needs' of the deceased."

42. A. Niwiński, "The Book of the Dead in the Coffins of the 21st Dynasty," in *Totenbuch-Forschungen: gesammelte Beiträge des 2. Internationalen Totenbuch-Symposiums 2005*, ed. B. Backes, I. Munro, and S. Stöhr (Wiesbaden, 2006), 263.

43. Both the motifs of the cow emerging and the tree goddess ended after the 21st Dynasty, and likely relating to a shift in the local traditions.

44. Niwiński, "Book of the Dead," 263. "Numerous offering scenes on the coffins may correspond to the real (or symbolical) visits paid during the burial procession to various chapels, where the objects of adoration may have been: sacred ram, sacred falcon, etc."

45. The alternating scenes and texts on the left side of the coffin correlate well. However, on the right side of the coffin, the texts and scenes do not exhibit such an obvious relationship.

46. Niwiński, *21st Dynasty Coffins from Thebes*, plate XVI.a.

47. Niwiński, *Book of the Dead*, 263.

48. A. Niwiński, *La seconde trouvaille de Deir el-Bahari*, Catalogue général des antiquités égyptiennes du Musée de Caire (Cairo, 1996). See scenes of the tree goddess and Hathor emerging from the desert in figure 23 (CG 6048) and figurer 34 (CG 6059); both are at the foot of the coffin, as they are here.

49. G. Daressy, *Cercueils des cachettes royales*, Catalogue général des antiquités égyptiennes du Musée du Caire (Cairo, 1909).

50. R. Egner and E. Hauslauer, *Särge der Dritten Zwischenzeit*, Corpus Antiquitatum Aegyptiacarum, Kunsthistorisches Museum Wien 10 (Mainz/Rhein, 1994), ÄS 6267a, 175–89.

GENEALOGY OF THE 21ST DYNASTY

Peter Lacovara

This is a simplified genealogy of the 21st Dynasty based on what we currently know. There are still many unanswered questions about this period and some of the relationships between these individuals are uncertain. The New Kingdom came to an end with the last king of the 20th Dynasty, Ramesses XI, who had no male heirs. The high priests of Amun at Karnak had already been challenging Ramesses XI. As a result, several powerful figures vied for control of Egypt.

After Ramesses XI's death, it appears that the high priest of Amun at Karnak, Pinedjem I, and Smendes, a local ruler at Tanis in the Delta, married the late king's daughters to assert their right to the throne.

Civil war was averted though diplomatic marriage and eventually the high priests of Amun at Thebes recognized Psusennes I, the son of Pinedjem I and Henuttawy, Ramesses XI's daughter by Queen Tentamun I. Though descended from the high priests of Thebes, Psusennes I ruled from and was buried at Tanis, and sons and successors followed suit. Rival Delta families also challenged the rule of the kings at Tanis, which included the Bubastite kings of the 22nd Dynasty, the Libyan kings of the 23rd Dynasty, and the Saite rulers of the 24th Dynasty. Again, marriages tied these families together so that open warfare did not break out, but it left Egypt weak and open to foreign invasion.

ANKHEFENMUT'S TUNIC

Peter Lacovara

During a close examination of Ankhefenmut's mummy and coffin, several bundles and numerous loose pieces of linen were discovered underneath the mummy. With the help of textile conservator Patricia Ewer and two textile specialists, Albany Institute

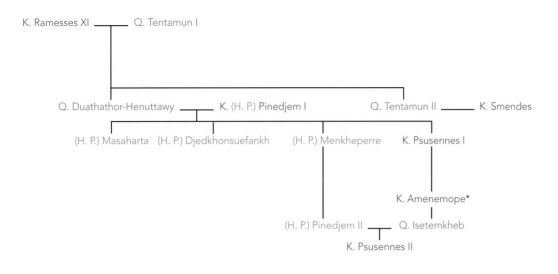

Thebes   Tanis

K. = Kings   Q. = Queens   H. P. = High Priests of Amun

*Also ruling at this time in the Delta were kings of Libyan origin, K. Osorkon the Elder and his successor and possibly son, Siamun.

board member Karen Nicholson and her colleague Kathleen Munn, we were able to undertake a thorough examination of the textile remains, revealing some surprising results.

The largest bundle (figure 50), when it was carefully unfolded, revealed evidence of an armhole, neckline, belt holes, and decorative fringe at the bottom. The next step was to determine the type of garment and its function. After several months of research and consultation with experts, the garment was determined to be a cassock, or tunic (figure 51), often referred to as a *kalasiris* by the ancient Greeks. These were worn as an everyday article of clothing by both sexes, especially by members of the upper classes.

The institute's example was made from a wide piece of linen fabric that still preserves a seam on one side, made by whip stitching the edges together. Belt holes were woven into the waist and decorative stitching around the neck. This tunic could be worn under an outer pleated linen robe or cloak, as illustrated on Ankhefenmut's coffin. The linen was usually left its natural color, because it was difficult to dye, although sometimes it has a yellowish tinge due to the starch used to iron pleats into it.

Also found in the coffin was another long piece of linen, possibly a shawl, which had a blue edge. The blue was from an indigo dye derived from a species of bean

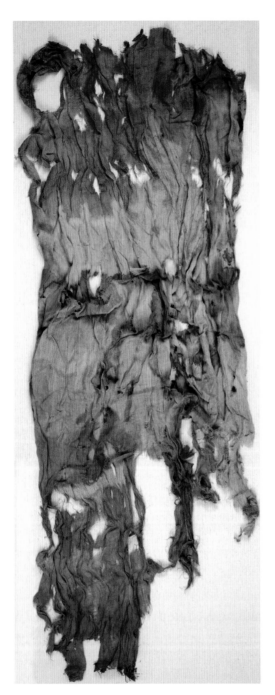

FIGURE 50. Ancient Egyptian tunic. Third Intermediate Period, 21st Dynasty, ca. 1069–945 BC. AIHA, gift of Samuel W. Brown, 1909.18.3. The remains of the tunic, now unfolded.

FIGURE 51. Reconstruction drawing of Ankhefenmut's tunic (in white). Illustration by Tom Nelson.

found in India. It was one of the few natural colors used to tint linen. It first appeared in Egypt and the Near East around the time Ankhefenmut lived. This fashion is even recorded in the Bible, in Numbers 15:38:

"Speak unto the children of Israel, and bid them that they make them fringes in the borders of their garments throughout their generations, and that they put upon the fringe of the borders a ribbon of blue."

THE CONSERVATION OF THE COFFIN OF ANKHEFENMUT

Leslie Ransick Gat and Erin Toomey

The coffin base of Ankhefenmut was cleaned and conserved in preparation for the *Mystery of the Albany Mummies* exhibition. As far as is known, the coffin had not been treated since its excavation in Egypt over a century ago.

The coffin was fabricated from boards of irregular shape, cut from a local softwood, and assembled together (figure 52). The joins and overall form of the coffin were refined by carving and sanding, and the wood was covered with layers of gesso ground, paint, and varnish. The coffin was found to be quite well preserved overall when it was examined prior to treatment. However, the shifting and opening of the original joins between the boards over thousands of years caused damage and losses to the gesso and polychrome. Our treatment focused primarily on stabilizing these joins and the loosened material surrounding them to prevent further

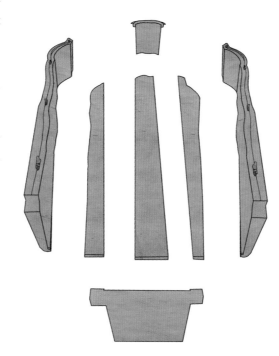

FIGURE 52. The boards that make up the coffin. Diagram by Sebastian Gat.

FIGURE 53. An open crack between the bottom and side panels of the coffin.

damage and loss. We would then integrate the areas of loss, not to create a "perfect" surface but to minimize areas thought to be visually distracting. What follows is a summary of that treatment.

Once the mummy had been removed from the coffin, fragments of textiles and other degraded burial material were gathered from the interior and saved for study. The interior surfaces were then vacuumed and brushed, and a large amount of decayed material was removed from the cracks and open joins located at the bottom of the coffin. The cleaning revealed traces of a figure painted on the bottom surface (see above), now only faintly legible due to deterioration. The rest of the interior was painted with a uniform red ochre that exhibited some water staining.

The exterior surfaces of the coffin were cleaned with particular care because the instability of the polychrome and gesso layers. Crystals that had formed over the interior and exterior sides of a small area of the coffin were removed during cleaning. Microchemical tests indicated the strong presence of chloride salts in these crystals, a common agent of deterioration, which can leach into buried objects from chloride-rich soils.

The unstable joins associated with the coffin base, including an almost completely detached bottom panel (figure 53), as well as additional cracks and other opened joins throughout, were cleaned as possible and consolidated so as to strengthen the wood in preparation for applying adhesives. Figure 54 shows damage to the polychrome due to movement of the wood.

FIGURE 54. Losses to the poly-chrome have occurred as a result of movement of the wood.

FIGURE 55. The coffin is clamped and the adhesive allowed to set.

FIGURE 56. Structural fills (the white material in the photo) associated with the join openings.

FIGURE 57. The fills shown in Figure 56 have been integrated with paint.

Once the joins were adhered and the elements clamped in place (figure 55), gaps associated with the joins were filled using Japanese tissue paper and putty to ensure that the joins were as secure as possible (figure 56). The structured fills were inpainted with acrylic paints to help visually recreate the original painted surface (figure 57). Finally, flaking polychrome was consolidated to create a flat surface and minimally inpainted with acrylic paint to hide paint losses.

As always, the coffin must be monitored regularly to make sure it remains stable. Large fluctuations in temperature and humidity are a wooden object's worst enemy. It is our hope that the newly stabilized coffin is now well positioned to continue its journey through time.

The Mummy of Ankhefenmut
A Scientific Investigation

Bob Brier, Phuong N. Vinh, Michael Schuster, Howard Mayforth, and Emily Johnson Chapin

Sir Flinders Petrie, the eccentric British Egyptologist, is often credited with founding the field of scientific Egyptology. He was not just interested in beautiful objects to decorate museums but realized that seemingly insignificant pottery fragments could be used to date archaeological sites. In 1897, Petrie excavated an ancient Egyptian cemetery at Deshasheh and X-rayed the feet and legs of a mummy. Although he published the X-ray images at the end of the volume he wrote about the excavation,[1] Petrie didn't mention them in the text. Perhaps just as the book was going to press, he had a chance to use the new technology and hurriedly inserted the illustration at the end.

The first mummy of a pharaoh was X-rayed in 1903 by Howard Carter, the discoverer of Tutankhamun's tomb. Carter and anatomist G. Elliot Smith took the mummy of Tuthmosis IV in a cab to the only hospital in Cairo with X-ray facilities. Later, as more hospitals acquired the right equipment, it became standard practice to X-ray a mummy under study. The great virtue of radiology for mummies is that it is nondestructive. No longer was it necessary to unwrap a mummy to see what was beneath the bandages. X-rays were an important step in mummy studies, but the field took a giant leap forward with the invention of CT scans.

Short for computer-assisted tomography, a CAT or CT scan is a series of X-ray cross-sections that can provide a complete record of a mummy. Once these images are loaded onto a computer (unlike standard X-rays, no film is used), sophisticated software manipulates the images, allowing the mummy to be viewed from any angle. When we began our examination of the mummy of Ankhefenmut, we knew that our primary tool would be the CT scan.

FIGURE 58. Mummy of Ankh-efenmut. Third Intermediate Period, 21st Dynasty, ca. 1069–945 BC. Linen, resin, and human remains. Bab el-Gasus. AIHA, gift of Samuel Brown, 1909.18.1a.

Two mummies have resided in the Albany Institute of History & Art for more than a century, but their first scientific study took place in 1989, and it was brief. When the mummies arrived from Egypt in 1909, each was in its own coffin. One was completely wrapped (figure 58) and in a coffin inscribed with the occupant's name and titles: Ankh-efenmut, priest in the temple of the goddess Mut and temple sculptor. The second mummy arrived unwrapped to the waist in the bottom of a black coffin of the Ptolemaic Period. For seventy-five years, the mummies remained in their coffins until their first scientific examination, when both were CT scanned. During that brief examination, it was tentatively suggested that the wrapped mummy was female and thus could not have been Ankhefenmut. Because of this tentative identification, it was believed that somehow during the mummies' early history their coffins were switched; the female, wrapped mummy belonged in the black coffin bottom and the partially unwrapped male mummy belonged in the coffin bottom inscribed for Ankhefenmut. This is where things stood for twenty-five years until 2012, when the mummies were being prepared for *The Mystery*

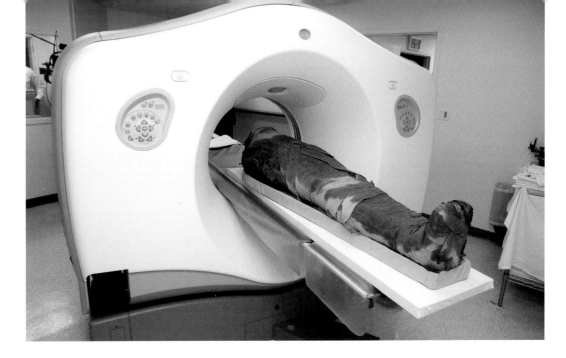

FIGURE 59. The wrapped mummy in the CT scanner.

of the Albany Mummies exhibition. At that time Dr. Peter Lacovara, guest curator for the planned exhibition, examined the mummies and noted that their wrappings did not chronologically match their now switched coffins. The mummy now in the inscribed 21st Dynasty coffin (1069–945 BC) had wrappings typical of a mummy of the later Ptolemaic Period (330–30 BC). The completely wrapped "female mummy," now in the black coffin bottom, had wrappings consistent with the date of the coffin inscribed for Ankhefenmut in which it had originally left Egypt. Thus, although the sex of the wrapped mummies now seemed right, the wrappings now seemed wrong. With this revelation as background, it was decided to conduct a thorough reexamination of both mummies with the primary objective of determining their sexes, ages at death, and any other characteristics that might help identify them.

The first step was to CT scan and X-ray the two mummies.[2] This was done at the Albany Medical Center. The CT scans were done on a GE LightSpeed 16 Slice scanner capable of producing high-resolution images (figure 59). The thin axial slices generated from the CT scan allow for two-dimensional (2D) reformatted and three-dimensional (3D) images to enhance visualization of the mummy's anatomy.

One of the primary objectives of our study was to determine the sex of the mummy who was believed to be male in 1909 but then thought to be female in 1989 as a result of the preliminary scientific study. Each day, we make numerous subconscious determinations about the sex of people we encounter. Often these decisions are based on clothes, length of hair, height, and so on. Sometimes more subtle cues, such as musculature and facial features, are necessary. Our mummy had no visible clothes or hair, and muscles were not available for viewing, so our study became something of a "CSI Egypt" investigation, using only the limited

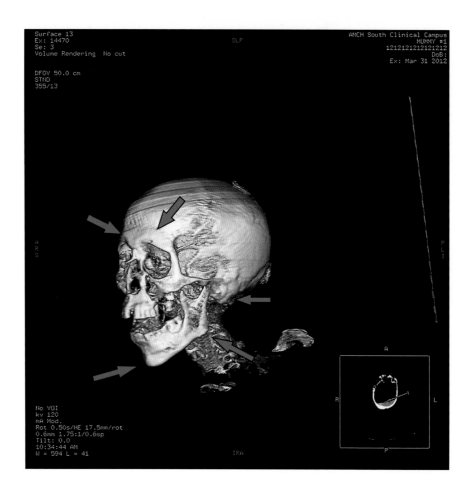

FIGURE 60. Three-dimensional CT scan of the facial bones and skull, showing distinctly male features. The two upper arrows show prominent supraorbital (brow) ridges. The horizontal arrow on the right shows a prominent mastoid process, a bony prominence behind the ear. The bottom left arrow shows a prominent square chin, and the bottom right arrow shows a sharp angular mandible (jaw bone).

clues a mummy presents. Fortunately, there were plenty of them.

Bones are a good indication of sex, and the CT scan gave us a wonderfully detailed picture of the skeletal structure. Males are generally more muscular than females. This includes the larger muscles of the legs and arms, such as the quadriceps, biceps, and triceps, as well as facial muscles. These muscles influence the bones to which they are attached. As muscles increase in size (through daily use, work, or specific physical training), the bones associated with them thicken to allow for insertion of more muscle tissue. Thus males tend to have thicker,

more robust bones and females have thinner, more gracile bones.

Robustness is not the only skeletal feature we can use to determine sex. The shapes of bones also help distinguish male from female. Generally males have more angular bones, and females more curved ones. This is most evident in the pelvis, but is also easily detected in cranial and facial bones. Males have more angular jaws and orbits of the eyes than do females, and they have more pronounced brows (supraorbital ridges). All of these features, taken together, often indicate the sex of a mummy.

As we examined the CT scans and X-rays of the mummy, a clear picture emerged. With our improved images, we were able to go far beyond the 1989 preliminary study. The first clues were in the face. The 3D scans showed male features. The mandible is robust and square. In addition, the ramus of the mandible—the part of the jaw that articulates with the bottom of the skull at the occipital condyles—forms nearly a right angle, another clue that our mummy is a male (figure 60). The supraorbital ridges are prominent, again indicating that the mummy is male, but even clearer is the mastoid process, a bony protuberance at the base of

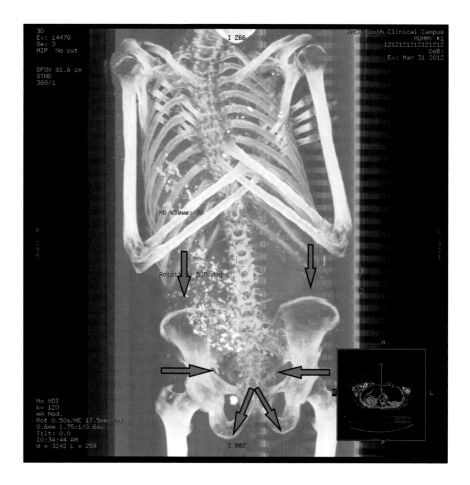

the skull. It is larger for males than for most females, and the mummy had quite a large mastoid process. The head of the mummy indicated male; what about the rest of him?

A female pelvis is quite different from that of a male, to allow for childbirth. In females, the pelvis is tilted toward the front. Also, it is shaped like a circle, whereas the male pelvis is less curved and is shaped like a smile. Radiologic analysis of the bony pelvis showed characteristic male features. The pelvic outlet has a smile configuration, rather than a broad oval, and the iliac crests are raised and narrow, rather than flat and broad (figure 61). There was one additional confirmation of the sex of our mummy. The front view showed a narrow (less than 90 degrees) subpubic angle. Finally, the 3D images of the pelvis revealed a narrow sciatic notch and an absence of the periauricular sulcus (a groove on the pelvis)—both male traits. The masculine pelvic contours were further confirmed by the robustness of the femurs (thigh bones), the longest bones in the body, so with almost 100 percent certainty we can say that this mummy is male.

With the sex of the mummy determined as male, we knew that he could indeed be Ankhefenmut the temple priest, but was

there any additional evidence besides sex that could support this identification? Our clue was that he was a sculptor. If he spent much of his time carving statues of the gods, then he would have repeatedly hefted a mallet and sent it crashing down on a chisel as he carved—which might lead to an asymmetry between his shoulders. The axial CT image through the right shoulder showed moderate changes of degenerative arthritis, with bone spurs and remodeling of the scapula. (This was not present in the left shoulder.) The shoulder, not being a weight-bearing joint like the hip or knee, is a less common joint to be involved by

FIGURE 61. Three-dimensional CT scan of bony pelvis with male features. The two vertical arrows show narrow and vertically oriented iliac wings, a male feature. The two horizontal central arrows outline the pelvic inlet, the opening to the pelvis. The pelvic inlet is narrowed and heart shaped, a male feature. The angle between the two lower arrows forms the infrapubic angle, which is acute, that is, less than 90 degrees, also a male feature.

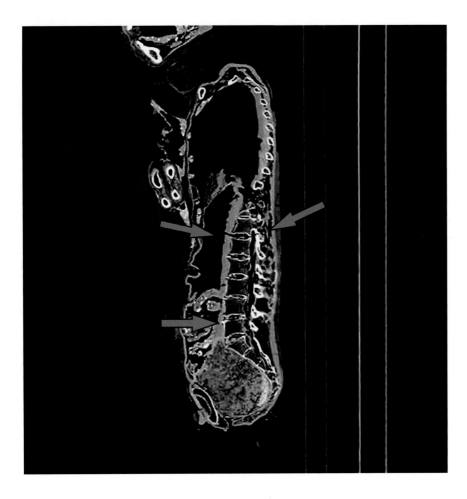

FIGURE 62. Two-dimensional sagittal lumbar CT scan. The upper left arrow shows a fracture through the front of the spine at the T12–L1 level. Note the fracture also through the hardened resin overlying the front of the spine. The right upper arrow indicates that the fracture has extended through to involve the supporting structures in the back of the spine (the posterior elements). The fracture has the features of the so-called Chance fracture. There are bone spurs at multiple levels of the lumbar spine, a finding seen in middle age. The left lower arrow shows a bone spur in the lumbar spine at the L5 vertebral body level.

degenerative arthritis, unless it is related to an occupation (such as a sculptor). If this is the case, the right side of his upper body should have been more muscular than the other, and this asymmetry should manifest itself by the bones of one side being more robust than those of the other. Indeed, the right scapula was more robust than the left, suggesting both that the mummy could have been a sculptor and that he was right handed. Although the evidence is consistent with our mummy being Ankhefenmut, we will never be certain, but it is a good bet that he really belongs in the decorated coffin in which he once again resides. With his

sex almost conclusively determined and his identity indicated with a modest degree of probability, we examined the CT scans and X-rays to see what else we could learn about him.

By looking at the long bones, we could tell something about our sculptor's diet— he ate well. His bones are well mineralized, solid, and uniform, indicating that his diet contained adequate protein and calcium. His teeth were also quite good, with no cavities or tooth loss. He was not a tall male: approximately 5 feet, 1.75 inches tall, which was not extremely short for an ancient Egyptian but well below the average of about 5 feet, 5 inches for males.

We were interested in finding out how old he was at the time of death, and we looked at several indicators. The ends of the long bones could indicate whether he died before middle age. When we are young, the ends of the bones, called the epiphyses, are not completely ossified and fused to the shafts of the bones. Ankhefenmut's bones were fully fused, so we know he was older than his twenties when he died, but how much older?

His spine showed the wear and tear of a middle-aged male. In the CT images, we can spot moderate degenerative changes in the spine, manifested by disk-space narrowing at multiple levels and bone spurs (figure 62). The images revealed moderate degenerative arthritis of both hips and knees, with calcification in the cartilage of the knee—typical of middle age. There were some bone spurs on the head and neck of the femurs, with the right showing more arthritis (figure 63). This asymmetry may be related to altered biomechanics in walking caused by the absence of the big toe (see below).

One more age indicator—cranial sutures—confirmed the picture of Ankhefenmut's age. The skull is made of several bones that knit together at places called sutures. As humans age, the sutures become more tightly knit, and this process continues into advanced age, when they are sometimes so tight that one can barely see them. Our mummy's sutures were knit to a degree that confirmed the other indicators of middle age.

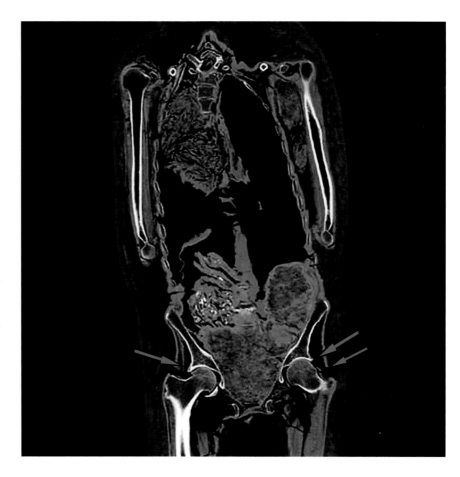

Another confirmation of this came from his bone density. As we grow older, our bones demineralize and become less dense. Ankhefenmut's remains show no signs of demineralization, so he was probably no older than fifty-five. We can thus estimate his age at death between fifty and fifty-five.

FIGURE 63. Two-dimensional coronal CT scan of the hips. There are bone spurs involving both hip joints, larger on the right, compatible with osteoarthritis, a finding seen in middle age. The larger, left-sided arrow shows bone spurs of the right hip joint, and the two smaller arrows show bone spurs of the left hip joint.

THE MISSING TOE

The CT scans and X-rays helped us determine sex and gave us a picture of Ankhefenmut's health, but perhaps the most interesting revelation was the fact that he had an artificial big toe on his right foot. It is not clear how he lost the toe, but the radiographs showed signs of avascular necrosis (bone death) of the sesamoid bone, a condition that

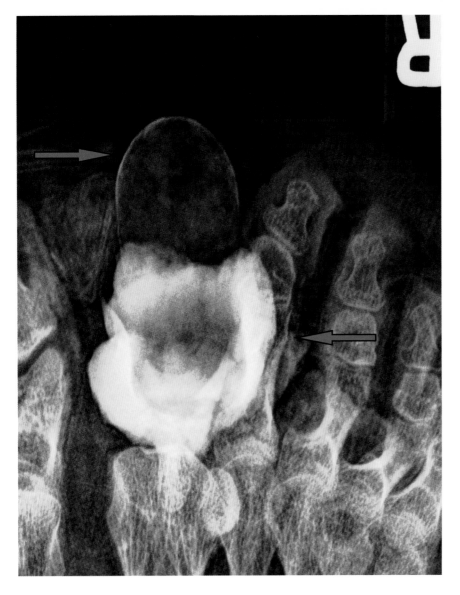

FIGURE 64. X-ray of the great toe prosthesis, which has two components. The upper left arrow shows the darker (more lucent) wooden component, and the lower right arrow shows the whiter (more dense) ceramic component.

would have caused some pain and suffering, but probably not enough for amputation.

In the 1989 investigation, the team noticed the artificial toe on the CT scans but were not sure what to make of it. Based on its density on the scans, they noted that it seemed to be made of a ceramic material and wondered if it was worn during Ankhefenmut's lifetime or was merely intended to make him whole in the next world. We hoped that with the

new CT scans we would be able to get better images and solve the mystery.

It is well known that embalmers occasionally supplied a substitute body part if one was missing, with the idea that the deceased would enjoy a fuller life in the next world. These artificial limbs were often necessitated by carelessness in the embalming workshops. One mummy in the Field Museum of Natural History in Chicago is clearly such a case. When it was X-rayed, it was discovered to have two heads, one in the usual place and one between the knees.[3] The best guess is that the head of some other mummy fell off in the embalmer's shop and some unconscientious worker just stuck it with another mummy. When the mummy was finally wrapped, who would know? One mummy in the Egyptian Museum in Cairo is practically skeletal, with some of its bones out of anatomical order and both hands and the right foot missing. The missing hands and foot were replaced with linen dummies, so clearly these were not worn during life.[4]

In the 1989 scan of our mummy, it was clear that the artificial toe was not a hastily fashioned substitute. With this as background, we scanned the ceramic toe.

The X-ray of the prosthetic toe clearly shows two distinct components, as seen in the different radiodensities of the two materials (figure 64). The part articulating with the foot appears to be ceramic, whereas the second component is thin and made of wood. A thin layer of resin coats the edge of the wood component. It is not easy to understand how this artificial toe would have worked. The ceramic part was placed against the remaining bones of the right foot and would have caused irritation. Could the toe really have been used in life? Or was it an embalmer's concoction so the deceased would be whole in the next world? Fortunately, there are two other artificial toes from ancient Egypt with which we can compare the Albany toe.

THE BRITISH MUSEUM TOE

The first of the two toes has been in the British Museum since 1891, when it was purchased from Rev. Greville Chester, who bought it in Egypt.[5] Unfortunately, we have no context for this artificial toe and know neither the specific location where it was found nor for whom it was made. Even so, it is a fascinating object. Made of cartonnage, a kind of papier mâché made of linen coated with plaster that was then painted, it is quite lifelike, even though it is now missing the toenail (figure 65).

Two sets of holes, eight along the longer, outer edge and four on the inner edge, were used to attach the prosthesis to the foot. The straps of traditional Egyptian sandals would have helped keep the toe in place. Given this artificial toe's design, it appears that it was used in real life.

THE VALLEY OF THE NOBLES TOE

The second ancient Egyptian artificial toe was discovered in 1998 by the German Archaeological Institute while they were excavating Tomb 95 in the Valley of the Nobles, on the west bank of the Nile opposite Luxor.[6] This toe was still attached to its owner, a badly damaged mummy of a middle-aged female from the 21st or 22nd Dynasty (1069–715 BC),

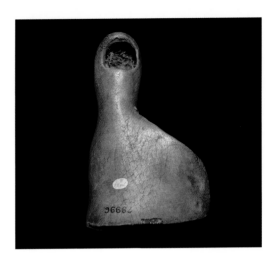

and is thus older than the British Museum's prosthetic toe and more finely crafted. It, too, replaced the big toe of the right foot. X-rays showed that the female's toe had been amputated during her lifetime, because the bone was covered by an intact layer of soft tissue and skin. The artificial toe was made of three wood pieces held together by seven leather laces. The largest piece was a realistically carved toe and toenail that was tied to two smaller wood plates. A piece of textile (foreground of figure 66) went across the wood plates and around the foot, holding the ensemble in place. Careful examination of the wood plates revealed signs of wear, so, like the British Museum toe, this one was also almost certainly used in life.

AN EXPERIMENT

Recently an experiment was conducted to see if either the British Museum toe or the one found in the Valley of the Nobles were true prosthetics used during the person's life.[7] Dr. Jacqueline Finch of Manchester University had replicas made of both artificial toes and found two living volunteers who were missing their right big toes to try out the prostheses. These volunteers wore replica Egyptian sandals over the toes to approximate ancient Egyptian conditions. Both toes performed extremely well. Each volunteer found the three-part wood toe the more comfortable, but one volunteer's foot mechanics were extremely efficient when wearing the replica cartonnage toe. From this study, it is reasonable to conclude that both prostheses served their ancient owners well in life. With this as background, we were in a better position to draw some conclusions about the Albany toe.

The Albany toe is made of material quite different from the two other known artificial toes. The other two are fashioned of wood, leather, and cartonnage—materials compatible with being worn in life—but the Albany toe, with its ceramic component, doesn't seem suitable for real life. Furthermore, for a prosthesis to be useful, it is usually fashioned to resemble the body part it replaces. The size of the Albany prosthetic is significantly larger than a normal big toe. The relatively fragile materials of the prosthesis and the lack of attachment sites on it demonstrate that the purpose of the toe was to make the deceased whole in the next world, rather than help him walk in this one.

THE MUMMIFICATION OF ANKHEFENMUT

Much of what we know about ancient Egypt comes from the study of mummies, and much of it relates to religion. The Egyptians were resurrectionists; they believed that the body was literally going to get up and go again in the next world, so it was crucial to preserve it. One reason they built tombs and filled them with their worldly belongings was that they believed they could take it all with them. The beautifully painted coffins with the names and titles of the deceased were an attempt to protect the mummy and also make sure that Osiris, lord of the Netherworld, knew who the person was when they arrived on his doorstep. The purpose of mummification, of course, was to preserve the body for resurrection.

There were various classes of mummification in ancient Egypt, depending on what you could afford. No matter what type of procedure was performed on the deceased, the goal was the same—dehydrate the body as quickly as possible. Bacteria will not attack soft tissue that does not contain water. This is why we can have dried fruits in our cereals: no water, no decay. The brain and the internal organs are especially moist, so if you could afford to pay for it, embalmers removed them.

Since the body you had in this world was the one you would have in the next world, the embalmers wanted to do as little damage as possible during mummification. For this reason, the internal organs were taken out through a small (about ten centimeters) incision in the left side of the abdomen. The brain was removed via the nasal passages by inserting a tool shaped like a miniature

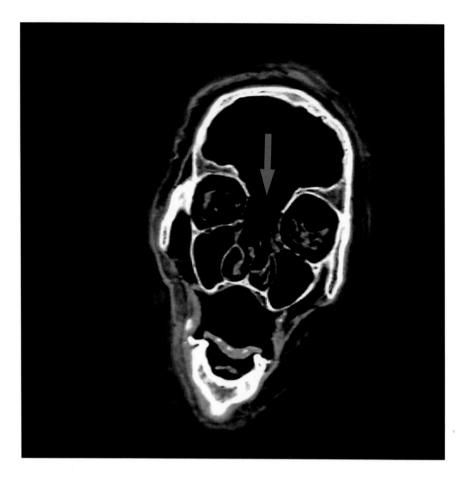

FIGURE 67. Two-dimensional coronal CT scan of the sinus. The vertical arrow shows a defect in the ethmoid bones to allow removal of the brain.

harpoon into the nostrils and tapping it to break through the ethmoid bone and enter the cranial cavity. An instrument resembling an opened metal coat hanger was inserted through the nasal passage into the cranium and rotated like a kitchen whisk to break down and liquefy the brain. The cadaver was turned upside down so the brain could run out through the nose. With the internal organs and brain removed, the next step was to dehydrate the rest of the body, especially the muscles.

The body was covered with natron, a naturally occurring compound of salt and baking soda (sodium bicarbonate) that drew out the rest of the body's liquids. After thirty days, the body was sufficiently dehydrated for wrapping. Often, the dehydrated internal organs were placed in four canopic jars so the mummy would have its organs in the next world. After the 20th Dynasty, Egyptians realized that tomb robbers frequently ransacked these jars looking for gold and destroyed the organs. By the 21st Dynasty, they placed the dehydrated internal organs back inside the abdominal cavity to protect them and then wrapped the mummy.

When the Greek historian Herodotus visited Egypt in 450 BC, he was told about three classes of mummification, depending on the status of the deceased. Sometimes the brain was not removed and the organs were left intact. We were curious to see if we could reconstruct the mummification of Ankhefenmut. Was it consistent with his status and the period during which he lived? The CT scans and X-rays would help us determine this.

The reformatted image of the nasal area shows clear evidence of the ancient embalmer's work. The hole through which the brain was removed was made with the goal of causing as little damage as possible. The ethmoid bones and the upper nasal cavity on the left have been pierced, but the damage is limited to this area, showing care and skill in removing the brain (figure 67). (Modern-day neurosurgeons do some brain surgery, such as removal of pituitary tumors, through the nose as well.) Further indications of the procedures used by the ancient embalmers came from the skull X-ray. The view of the back of the head showed that after the brain was removed, the embalmers poured hot resin into the cranium via the nasal passages to cauterize the area in case not all of the brain had been removed. The resin, now solidified, can clearly be seen on the scan (figure 68).

Scans of the abdominal area showed signs of mummification, which helped us establish the period during which Ankhenefmut lived. First we could see the embalmer's incision, through which the internal organs were removed, on the left side of the abdomen. It was in the traditional place and was the usual size, about 10.5 centimeters. Further examination of the scans showed four packets, almost certainly the internal organs placed back in the body. The practice of replacing the organs began around the 21st Dynasty, which is when Ankhefenmut lived.

Three of the packets were on the right side and one on the lower left, which makes sense when one thinks about the position of the incision. The embalmer knew he had four packets to fit into the body cavity. The

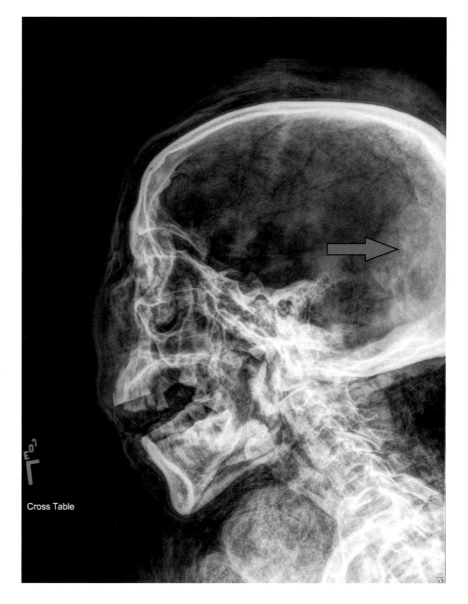

incision is on the left side, so we can imagine him with the first packet, reaching in and pushing it as far in as he can (to the right) to leave room for the other three. He did the same with the next two, and then, when he had only one left, he didn't have to push it all the way in to leave room for others, so he left it near the incision on the left side.

Close to the abdominal packets one can see bright specks on the scans. In a living

FIGURE 68. Resin poured into the cranium clearly visible at the back of the skull.

patient, such high-density small objects might indicate calcifications. With this mummy, they are almost certainly granules of natron, the salt compound used to dehydrate the internal organs.

An interesting incidental finding in this mummy is a so-called Chance fracture[8] of the thoracic and lumbar spine, extending through the T12–L1 disk space (mid to lower back). This serious fracture is today known as a "seat belt fracture" because it is seen in motor vehicle accidents with the passenger restrained in a seat belt or is seen in a fall from a significant height. In this mummy, the Chance fracture was clearly postmortem, probably due to being dropped by twentieth-century movers. In addition to the spine fracture, there were fractures seen in the adjacent hardened resin, but no other bony fractures were visible.

CONCLUSIONS

In science, we never reach absolute certainty, but the X-ray and CT scans of the wrapped mummy have enabled us to draw some conclusions with a fair degree of reliability. First, our mummy was a male. Second, his body is compatible with the occupation of temple sculptor, as stated on the coffin in which he arrived on the banks of the Hudson River more than a century ago. Third, we can reconstruct his mummification, from the removal of his brain to the replacement of his internal organs inside his abdominal cavity. Such mummification is consistent with the time period in which Ankhefenmut lived. The wrapped mummy is almost certainly Ankhefenmut, and he once again rests in the coffin made for him 2,500 years ago.

There was an ancient Egyptian saying: "To speak the name of the dead again is to make him live again." We hope Ankhefenmut would be pleased with our study.

NOTES

1. W. M. F. Petrie, *Deshasheh* (London, 1898), plate XXXVII.

2. The team that examined the mummies consisted of Bob Brier, senior research fellow, C.W. Post Campus, Long Island University, an Egyptologist specializing in mummies; radiologists Phuong Vinh, assistant professor of radiology, Albany Medical Center, and Michael Schuster, assistant professor of radiology, Albany Medical Center; and Howard Mayforth, radiologic technician, and Emily Johnson Chapin, X-ray technician, both of the Albany Medical Center.

3. R. L. Moodie, "Roentgenologic Studies of Egyptian and Peruvian Mummies," *Field Museum of Natural History, Anthropology Memoirs*, vol. 3 (Chicago, 1931).

4. P. H. K. Gray, "Embalmers' 'Restorations,'" *Journal of Egyptian Archaeology*, 52 (1966), 138–40.

5. N. Reeves, "New Light on Ancient Egyptian Prosthetic Medicine," in *Studies in Egyptian Antiquities: A Tribute to T. G. H. James*, ed. W. V. Davies (London, 1999), 73–77.

6. A. Nerlich et al., "Ancient Egyptian Prosthesis of the Big Toe," *Lancet*, 356 (December 23, 2000), 2176–79.

7. J. Finch, "Ancient Origins of Prosthetic Medicine," *Lancet*, 377 (February 12, 2011), 548–49.

8. First described in 1948 by G. Q. Chance.

Albany's Ptolemaic Mummy and Late Period Funerary Arts

Peter Lacovara

The second mummy that Samuel Brown purchased for Albany dates to a time much later than that of Ankhefenmut, sometime during the period when the family of Alexander the Great's general, Ptolemy, ruled the country. Unfortunately, the lid of the coffin containing this mummy was damaged and discarded in Cairo, so we do not know who this individual was or his occupation. His shaved head would certainly suggest that he served at least some of his time as a temple priest, as they had to be totally shaved to be ritually pure. He also had henna on his finger- and toenails, which would suggest a fairly high-status individual, as does the fine job of mummification. Like most mummies in the later periods of Egyptian history, his arms are crossed to equate him with Osiris, the god of the dead (figure 69). Sometimes the mummy's name would be written on a wooden tag so that its identity would not be lost in an embalmer's shop, where multiple bodies were being prepared (figure 70). The coffin base is decorated only with a crudely painted image of the Goddess of the West, the patroness of the cemetery (figure 71), and only one side has an inscription. Jonathan Elias, a scholar who has studied the funerary material of this period, has translated and commented on the texts written on the side of the coffin. The yellow text on the shallow, black-coated coffin bottom is a type known from Akhmim and elsewhere in Upper Egypt that became particularly prominent during the third century BC.[1]

The hieroglyphic signs making up the *hetep di nesewt* offering formula, which runs along the top outer edge of the proper left side of the coffin bottom, are arranged retrograde; that is, they begin just above the

FIGURE 69. Osiris. Late Period to Ptolemaic Period, ca. 664–30 BC. Bronze. AIHA, gift of Heinrich Medicus, 2013.1.2. Many votive images were made of the god of the Underworld, Osiris. He is usually depicted as he is here, wrapped as a mummy holding the crook and flail, with a divine beard and the elaborate headdress of horns and feathers known as the *atef* crown. On his back and side there are rings to attach to a chain so that the figure could be worn as an amulet around the neck but be held straight and kept from swinging. Osiris was the god of the dead, and Egyptians believed that when you died, you became a form of this deity. A deceased individual would be referred to as "the Osiris."

pedestal base of the coffin and face opposite to their expected direction. This backward writing is sometimes found on religious texts.

The text reads: "A gift-which-the-king-gives and Osiris, foremost of the west, great god, lord of Abydos, and Isis-the-great, mother of the god, and Nephthys, sister of the god, and Harendotes. . . ."

Harendotes was a form of the god Horus, "Horus protector of his father," who was worshipped at Akhmim and is often associated with the goddesses Isis or Nephthys. The inscription on this coffin is similar to other offering formulae found on Ptolemaic funerary stelae and coffins from Akhmim.[2] Unfortunately, the text does not record the name of the owner, and it may be that this was a generic coffin that was never inscribed due to lack of time or the illiteracy of those conducting the burial.

Mummies were sometimes covered with a network of faience beads, imitating the dress of the gods, in which the images of the Four Sons of Horus, a winged scarab, and even a mummy mask could be woven.[3] A variety of amulets were placed on the body to protect various parts of the mummy, such as the heart, backbone, and neck, and to ensure the mummy would enjoy a resurrection in the next life.

The Ptolemaic Period, like the Third Intermediate Period, was an era in which generally few objects were placed in the tomb with the mummy and coffin. One feature that began in Ankhefenmut's day and continued into the Ptolemaic Period was the inclusion of a copy of the Book of the Dead or another one of the magical texts known as the Underworld books in the tomb. These were often placed with a figure of the composite funerary god Ptah-Sokar-Osiris[4] (figure 72).

FIGURE 70. Mummy tag. Ptolemaic Period, ca. 305–30 BC. Wood. AIHA, gift of Sarah Paine Potter (Mrs. Howard B. Potter), 1934.4.8. This tag identifies a mummy with the name of the deceased and an image of the god Anubis.

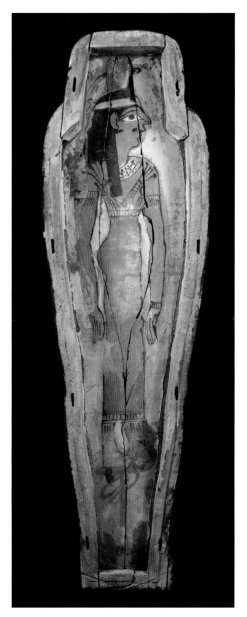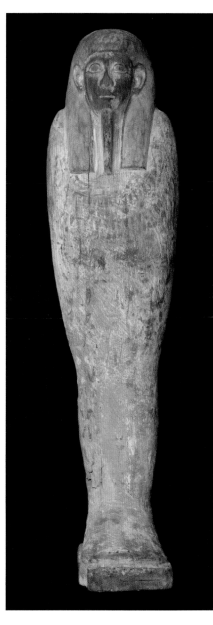

FIGURE 71. Base of coffin. Early Ptolemaic Period, ca. 305–200 BC. Wood and pigment. Akhmim. AIHA, gift of Samuel W. Brown, 1909.18.2b. The lid of this mummy's coffin did not make it back to Albany, but the base did. Typical of late Egyptian wooden coffins, this base is roughly made of irregular boards of local softwood. The inside of the bottom is painted with an image of the Goddess of the West, the patroness of the cemetery who would protect the mummy in the afterlife.

FIGURE 72. Ptah-Sokar-Osiris figure. Late Period, ca. 664–332 BC. Wood and pigment. AIHA, gift of Sarah Paine Potter (Mrs. Howard B. Potter), 1934.4.6. Several gods were often combined into a single deity with the powers of all. Ptah-Sokar-Osiris incorporated the qualities of the creator god Ptah, the solar god Sokar, and the Underworld god Osiris. Figures of this combined divinity first commonly appear in tombs of the 21st Dynasty and would have contained a rolled-up Book of the Dead in their long, rectangular bases.

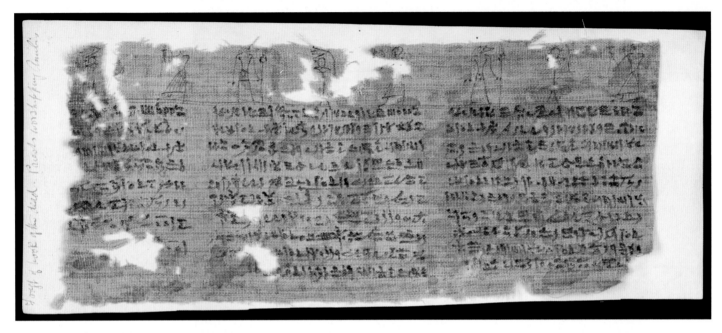

FIGURE 73. Book of the Dead of Nespasef. Late Period, 26th Dynasty, ca. 664–332 BC. Papyrus and ink. AIHA, gift of Miss Ellen Campbell, 1900.3.10. Any compilation of texts from the Book of the Dead served the same purpose: to ensure that the deceased "goes forth by day," meaning that they are reborn and attain eternal life. They were written on papyrus with black ink; red ink was sometimes used to mark new passages or important texts.

FIGURE 74. Mummy bandage with funerary text. Ptolemaic Period, ca. 305–30 BC. AIHA, gift of Miss Ellen Campbell, 1900.3.11. Sometimes the texts of the Book of the Dead were written directly in the mummy's bandages. This piece is inscribed for Pa-ti-Heka, son of Ta-sherit-n-ta-qry. Other examples of his bandages are known.

One of the first Egyptian objects to enter the collection at the Albany Institute is a portion of the Book of the Dead that belonged to a man named Nespasef[5] (figure 73). It is written on a long sheet of papyrus in red and black ink and had spaces for illustrations, which were never added. In composing the Book of the Dead, the scribes would write down select passages on papyrus sheets, which were decorated by artists who would add in the proper images and scenes. In the case of this particular papyrus, however, that never happened, and the spaces remained blank. The papyrus contains excerpts from chapters 20, 26, 27, 28, 29, 32, 33, 34, 35, 36, 37, 38, 40, and 42 of the Book of the Dead. Other fragments of this papyrus with additional texts have been identified in the collection of the Cincinnati Art Museum. Sometimes the text would be written directly on linen mummy bandages rather than papyrus, and an example in the Albany Institute has a short inscription illustrated by some lightly sketched figures (figure 74).

Many species of animals were mummified in the later periods of ancient Egypt. These were not pets but were sacred animals, often raised in temple precincts. The animals were sacrificed and mummified, some almost as elaborately as humans. They were left as offerings in temples by pious pilgrims, along with bronze votive figures of gods and goddesses. When a sufficient number of offerings had been collected in the temple, the figurines and animal mummies were gathered up and buried by the priests in sacred ground or in vast animal catacombs. Funerary stelae could even be set up for some of the animal mummies (figure 75).

All manner of animals could be mummified, including cats and dogs, ibises and falcons, monkeys, bulls, and even crocodiles, fish, snakes, and shrew-mice.[6] Sometimes the type of animal could be confused, as was the case with a cat mummy acquired by the Albany Institute of History & Art from the Metropolitan Museum of Art (figure 76a–b). In 2002, Dr. Douglas Cohn, a veterinarian and director of the Animal Resources Facility

FIGURE 75. Stela for a sacred ibis. Late Period to Ptolemaic Period, ca. 664–30 BC. AIHA, gift of Heinrich Medicus, 2013.1.20. This stela depicts a man playing the double pipes for a sacred ibis. A number of such stelae were found in the large cemetery of ibis mummies at Tuna el-Gebel in Middle Egypt.

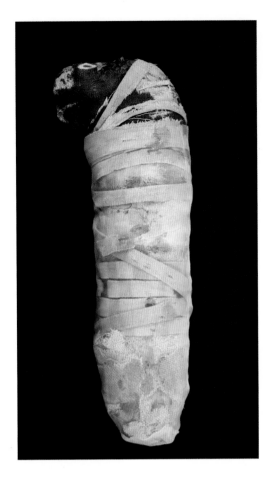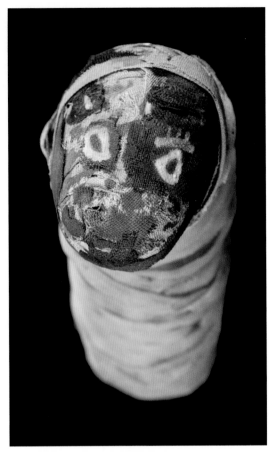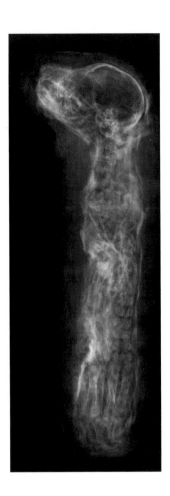

FIGURE 76. Dog mummy (a–b) and X-ray (c). Roman Period, ca. 30 BC–AD 395. Kharga Oasis. AIHA, 1958.7.4. This mummy of a small puppy was first thought to be a cat until it was X-rayed and examined at Albany Medical Center.

at Albany Medical College, suggested that the cat mummy undergo CT scans and X-rays (figure 76c). Based on the skull structure, the CT scans revealed that the "cat" was actually a dog![7]

NOTES

1. Jonathan Elias, personal communication.

2. J. Elias, *Production and Use in Elite Mortuary Preparation* (Ann Arbor, 1999).

3. See K. Bosse-Griffiths, "Some Egyptian Beadwork Faces in the Wellcome Collection at University College Swansea," *Journal of Egyptian Archaeology*, 66 (1978), 99–106.

4. M. J. Raven, "Papyrus-Sheaths and Ptah-Sokar-Osiris Statues," *Oudheidkundige Mededelingen uit het Rijksmuseum van Oudheden te Leiden*, 59–60 (Leiden, 1978–79), 251–96 and plates 39–41.

5. A. Niwiński, *Studies on the Illustrated Theban Funerary Papyri of the 11th and 10th Centuries B.C.* (Göttingen, 1989).

6. S. Ikram, ed., *Divine Creatures: Animal Mummies in Ancient Egypt* (Cairo, 2005).

7. T. Cahill, "It Took a CAT to Reveal that Mummy Is Really a Dog," *Albany Times Union*, March 6, 2003.

The Ptolemaic Mummy
A Scientific Investigation

Bob Brier, Phuong N. Vinh, Michael Schuster, Howard Mayforth, and Emily Johnson Chapin

We were able to identify Ankhefenmut with some certainty, but the second mummy brought with him to Albany in 1909 remains unidentified. This does not mean that we can't find out more about him. As with Ankhefenmut, through X-rays and CT scans we attempted to determine his age, sex, and the period during which he was mummified.[1]

It was easiest to determine the sex because his head is unwrapped and the facial features are clearly masculine (figure 77). Radiographs (figures 78a–b) confirm that his mandible (jaw) is angular and robust and his supraorbital (brow) ridges are pronounced. He also has a prominent mastoid process (a spiny protuberance at the base of the skull). The eye sockets are nearly rectangular, another masculine trait. In addition, the X-rays show his wrapped penis (figure 79), so we have no doubts that

he is a male. Even so, the mummy is a good example of something physical anthropologists are very aware of—many people have both masculine and feminine traits. Some women have square jaws, and some men have hardly any supraorbital (brow) ridges. The scans for this mummy showed a slightly feminine pelvis. Women have wider pelvises to facilitate childbirth; this mummy, though clearly a man, also has a wide pelvis and a wide greater sciatic notch (see figure 79), both generally considered feminine traits. This is why it is important to use as many indicators as possible when determining the sex of a mummy. If we had examined only the pelvic bones, we could have made a mistake.

We were able to see that all his molars had erupted, so it is almost certain that he was more than twenty-one years old when he

FIGURE 77. Mummy of a priest. Early Ptolemaic Period, ca. 305–200 BC. Akhmim. AIHA, gift of Samuel Brown, 1909.18.2a. The unknown Albany mummy arrived from Cairo partially unwrapped.

FIGURE 78. The facial characteristics of this mummy are typically male. The arrows in (a) show these traits: the arrow at the top indicates the pronounced supraorbital ridge; the lower arrow on the left side shows a square chin; and the one on the lower right shows a flared, angular gonion of the mandible. The orbits (eye sockets) in (b) are angular, another male trait.

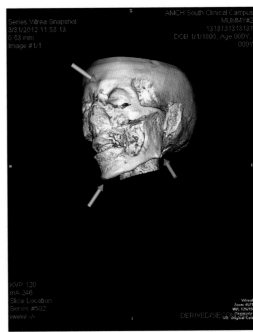

78a

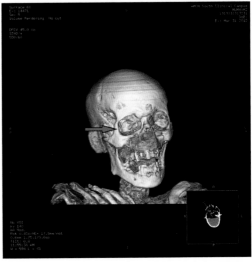

78b

died. This was confirmed by the epiphyses (ends) of the long bones, which the scans showed to be fully fused, a process that is completed around the age of twenty-one. This can also be seen in figure 79, where the ends of the femurs, the longest bones in the body, are fully fused. Cranial sutures gave us additional information about his age. They continue to close throughout life, and the degree of closure is consistent with someone in his forties. This estimate was confirmed by the X-rays of his spine, hips, and knees showing minor wear and arthritis, again consistent with someone who died in his forties. This can be seen in figure 80, especially in the right hip. So our unknown Albany mummy is definitely a male and died in his forties. The next step was to see if we could determine when he died.

Mummification techniques changed over the centuries, so if we could determine how he was preserved, it might be possible to determine the period in which he died. Our radiological images of the skull showed that the brain had been removed through the right nasal passages (figure 81). The scan shows that the ethmoid bone has been broken to gain entry to the cranium. Often the embalmers went in through both nasal passages, breaking the ethmoid bone on

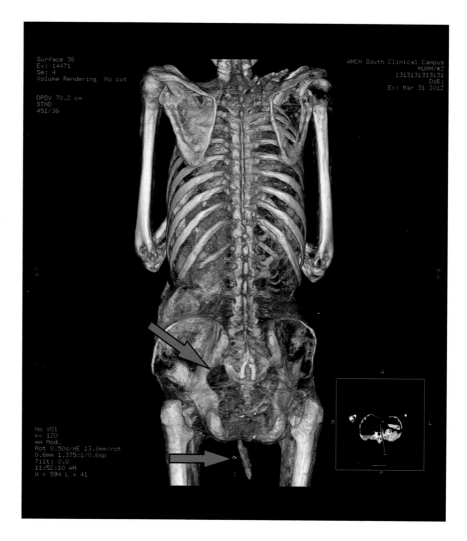

both sides. The fact that they entered only through one side shows great care in the mummification—they wanted to do as little damage as possible to the body.

After the brain was removed, the embalmers cauterized the cranial area by introducing hot resin through the right nasal passage. This resin cooled and solidified inside the skull, as can clearly be seen at the back of the head (figure 82). Scans of the mummy's abdominal cavity showed that his internal organs had been removed, desiccated, wrapped in linen, and replaced inside the

FIGURE 79. The mummy's wrapped penis (lower arrow) can be seen in the CT scan. Although he is clearly male, his pelvis is wide, somewhat feminine. The diagonal arrow points to a wide greater sciatic notch, a feminine trait.

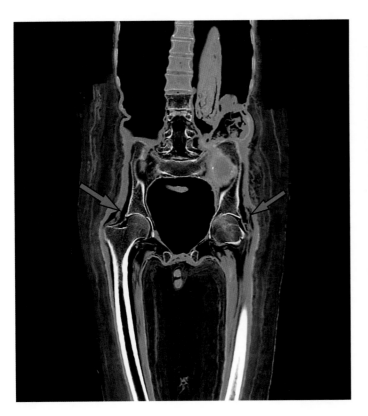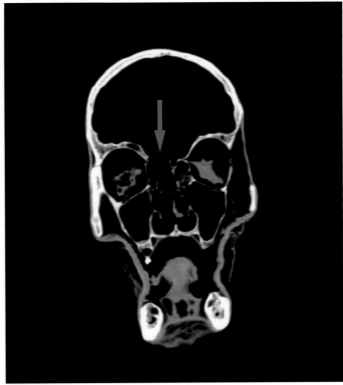

FIGURE 80. The two arrows show osteoarthritis of both hips, a feature of middle age. The arrow on the left side of the image corresponds to the right hip. On close inspection of the CT and X-rays, the right hip osteoarthritis was greater than that on the left. In a young person, there would be a horizontal line on the CT scan near the top of the femur, because the tip would not be fully fused with the rest of the bone.

FIGURE 81. The facial scan shows a defect in the roof of the right ethmoid air cells, allowing for removal of the brain via the nasal cavity.

body (figure 83). This practice of replacing the internal organs in the body began in the 21st Dynasty (1069–945 BC). We now knew that the Albany mummy lived sometime after 1069 BC, toward the end of ancient Egyptian history. When our mummy was alive, the pyramids were already 2,000 years old.

The mummy's wrappings enabled us to pinpoint when he lived a bit more precisely. The very fine crisscross wrappings were typical of the end of pharaonic Egypt, the Ptolemaic Period, when Greek kings named Ptolemy were in control (305–30 BC). The Albany mummy lived and died during this period.

We can also say something about his diet. His bones are well mineralized—meaning he had a healthful diet and was getting the minerals and protein needed for healthy bones. This can be seen from the CT scan of his long bones (see figure 80). Well-mineralized bones are more dense than those of people with poor diets and consequently appear whiter on CT scans. Although we may never know who the Albany Ptolemaic mummy is, we do know quite a lot about his age, status, and health.

One of the most striking features of this mummy is how he was partially unwrapped. From the head to the chest, the bandages have been removed so carefully that it looks as if a precision saw was used, leaving the remaining bandages in perfect condition. It is even possible to count the layers

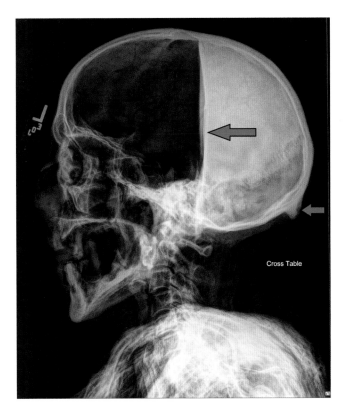

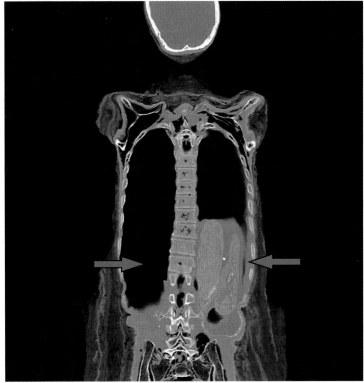

of wrappings (see figure 77). When did this unwrapping occur? In the mummy's 100-year history at the Albany Institute, there was never a time when it was shown totally wrapped. This leaves us to conclude that it was unwrapped in Cairo in the Egyptian Museum's sale room, to show potential customers what they were getting.

FIGURE 82. Resin was poured into the skull through the right nasal passage, and it later solidified. The upper, large arrow shows a layer of hardened resin in the back of the skull. The lower, smaller arrow points to a prominent occipital protuberance in the back of the skull, a male characteristic.

FIGURE 83. The smaller arrow on the left side of the image shows a dark area in the right side of the mummy's abdomen, corresponding to an empty space where the organs have been removed. The larger arrow on the right indicates dehydrated organs, wrapped and rolled up and packed within the abdominal cavity on the left side of the mummy.

NOTES

1. The team consisted of Bob Brier, senior research fellow, C.W. Post Campus, Long Island University; Phuong Vinh and Michael Schuster, assistant professor of radiology, Albany Medical Center; Howard Mayforth, radiologic technician, Albany Medical Center; and Emily Johnson Chapin, X-ray technician, Albany Medical Center.

EGYPTIAN ARTIFACTS

Book of the Dead of Nespasef. Late Period, 26th Dynasty, ca. 664–525 BC. Papyrus and ink, H. 36.20 cm. × W. 193.04 cm. (14 1/4 in. × 76 in.). Albany Institute of History & Art, gift of Miss Ellen Campbell, 1900.3.10.

Funerary cone. New Kingdom, 18th Dynasty, ca. 1550–1292 BC. Ceramic, H. 1.91 cm. × Dia. 7.62 cm. (3/4 in. × 3 in.). Albany Institute of History & Art, gift of J. Townsend Lansing, 1900.7.3.

Mummy bandage with funerary text. Ptolemaic Period, ca. 305–30 BC. Linen and ink, H. 10.16 cm. × W. 22.86 cm. (4 in. × 9 in.). Albany Institute of History & Art, gift of Miss Ellen Campbell, 1900.3.11.

Mummy of Ankhefenmut. Third Intermediate Period, 21st Dynasty, ca. 1069–945 BC. Linen, resin, and human remains, H. 36.20 cm. × L. 153.35 cm. × W. 22.23 cm. (14 1/4 in. × 3/8 in. × 8 3/4 in.). Bab el-Gasus, Egypt. Albany Institute of History & Art, gift of Samuel W. Brown, 1909.18.1a.

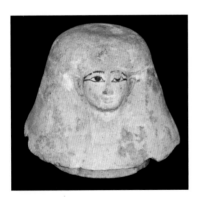

Canopic jar lid. New Kingdom, ca. 1550–1069 BC. Ceramic and pigment, H. 13.97 cm. × Dia. 14.61 cm. (5 1/2 in. × 5 3/4 in.). Albany Institute of History & Art, gift of Miss Ellen Campbell, 1900.3.12.

Base of Ankhefenmut's coffin. Third Intermediate Period, 21st Dynasty, ca. 1069–945 BC. Wood, gesso, and pigment, H. 47.63 cm. × L. 193.68 cm. × W. 26.99 cm. (18 3/4 in. × 76 1/4 in. × 10 5/8 in.). Bab el-Gasus, Egypt. Albany Institute of History & Art, gift of Samuel W. Brown, 1909.18.1b.

Mummy of priest. Early Ptolemaic Period, ca. 305–200 BC. Linen, resin, and human remains, H. 22.86 cm. × L. 185.42 cm. × W. 41.91 cm. (9 in. × 73 in. × 16 1/2 in.). Akhmim, Egypt. Albany Institute of History & Art, gift of Samuel W. Brown, 1909.18.2a.

Shawl with blue selvage. Third Intermediate Period, 21st Dynasty, ca. 1069–945 BC. Linen, H. 6.35 cm. × L. 43.18 cm. (2 1/2 in. × 17 in.). Albany Institute of History & Art, gift of Samuel W. Brown, 1909.18.4.

Coffin base with Goddess of the West. Early Ptolemaic Period, ca. 305–200 BC. Wood and pigment, H. 13.97 cm. × L. 175.26 cm. × W. 49.53 cm. (5 1/2 in. × 69 in. × 19 1/2 in.). Akhmim, Egypt. Albany Institute of History & Art, gift of Samuel W. Brown, 1909.18.2b.

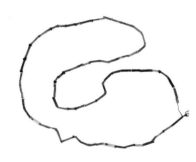

Ancient Egyptian necklace. New Kingdom to Late Period, ca. 1550–332 BC. Egyptian faience, H. 0.32 cm. × L. 71.12 cm. (1/8 in. × 28 in.). Albany Institute of History & Art, gift of Leontine deKay Townsend (Mrs. John Townsend) Lansing, 1930.8.1.

Ancient Egyptian tunic. Third Intermediate Period, 21st Dynasty, ca. 1069–945 BC. Linen, H. 41.91 cm. × L. 128.27 cm. (16 1/2 in. × 50 1/2 in.). Albany Institute of History & Art, gift of Samuel W. Brown, 1909.18.3.

Necklace. New Kingdom to Late Period, ca. 1550–332 BC. Stone, Egyptian faience, carnelian, and colored glass, H. 1.27 cm. × L. 20.32 cm. (1/2 in. × 8 in.). Albany Institute of History & Art, gift of J. Townsend Lansing, 1930.8.2.

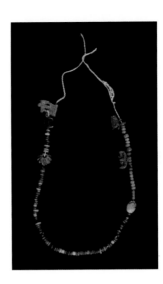

String of beads with three amulets. New Kingdom to Late Period, ca. 1550–332 BC. Egyptian faience, carnelian, and glass, H. 1.27 cm. × L. 41.91 cm. (1/4 in. × 16 1/2 in.). Albany Institute of History & Art, gift of J. Townsend Lansing, 1930.8.3.

Ptah-Sokar-Osiris figure. Late Period, ca. 664–332 BC. Wood and pigment, H. 40.01 cm. × W. 9.53 cm. × D. 6.99 cm. (15 3/4 in. × 3 3/4 in. × 2 3/4 in.). Albany Institute of History & Art, gift of Sarah Paine Potter (Mrs. Howard B. Potter), 1934.4.6.

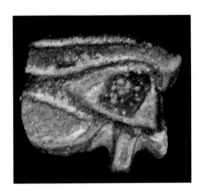

Wedjet-eye amulet. Late Period, ca. 664–332 BC. Egyptian faience, H. 2.2 cm. × W. 2.5 cm. × D. 0.64 cm. (3/4 in. × 1 in. × 1/4 in.). Albany Institute of History & Art, gift of J. Townsend Lansing, 1930.8.3a.

Sistrum handle. Ptolemaic Period, ca. 305–30 BC. Egyptian faience, H. 4.45 cm. × W. 3.18 cm. × D. 1.91 cm. (1 3/4 in. × 1 1/4 in. × 3/4 in.). Albany Institute of History & Art, gift of Sarah Paine Potter (Mrs. Howard B. Potter), 1934.4.7.

Shabti. Third Intermediate Period, ca. 1069–664 BC. Egyptian faience, H. 8.26 cm. × W. 2.54 cm. × D. 1.27 cm. (3 1/4 in. × 1 in. × 1/2 in.). Albany Institute of History & Art, gift of Sarah Paine Potter (Mrs. Howard B. Potter), 1934.4.5.

Mummy tag. Ptolemaic Period, ca. 305–30 BC. Wood, H. 1.91 cm. × W. 5.72 cm. × D. 0.64 cm. (3/4 in. × 2 1/4 in. × 1/4 in.). Albany Institute of History & Art, gift of Sarah Paine Potter (Mrs. Howard B. Potter), 1934.4.8.

Amulet mold of King Akhenaten. New Kingdom, 18th Dynasty, reign of Akhenaten, ca. 1352–1336 BC. Ceramic, H. 3.81 cm. × L. 3.81 cm. × D. 1.27 cm. (1 1/2 in. × 1 1/2 in. × 1/2 in.). Albany Institute of History & Art, gift of Mrs. Howard B. Paine, 1934.4.9.

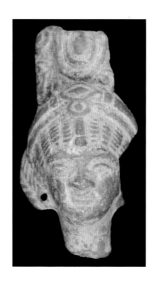

Head of Isis Fortuna. Early Roman Period, ca. first century AD. Ceramic, H. 7.62 cm. × W. 4.45 cm. × D. 3.81 cm. (3 in. × 1 3/4 in. × 1 1/2 in.). Albany Institute of History & Art, x1940.234. (new number 1934.4.16).

Cosmetic jar. First Intermediate Period, ca. 2160–2055 BC, or later. Alabaster, H. 6.35 cm. × greatest Dia. 5.08 cm. (2 1/2 in. × 2 in.). Albany Institute of History & Art, gift of Sarah Paine Potter (Mrs. Howard B. Potter), 1934.4.13.

Winged scarab. Late Period to Early Ptolemaic Period, ca. 664–200 BC. Ceramic and pigment, H. 6.99 cm. × W. 20 cm. × D. 0.64 cm. (2 3/4 in. × 7 7/8 in. × 1/4 in.). Albany Institute of History & Art, x1940.600.1006.

Jar. New Kingdom, 18th Dynasty, ca. 1550–1292 BC. Ceramic and pigment, H. 15.24 cm. × W. 9.53 cm. × Dia. 13.97 cm. (6 in. × 3 3/4 in. × 5 1/2 in.). Albany Institute of History & Art, x1940.225. (new number 1934.4.15).

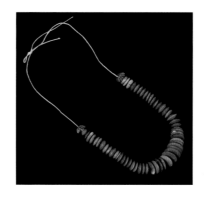

Necklace of disk beads. New Kingdom, ca. 1550–1069 BC. Egyptian faience and glass, H. 1.27 cm. × L. 13.97 cm. (1/2 in. × 5 1/2 in.). Albany Institute of History & Art, gift of J. Townsend Lansing, x1940.600.1009.6.

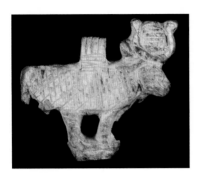

Cow amulet. New Kingdom, ca. 1550–1069 BC, or later. Steatite, H. 0.95 cm. × L. 2.22 cm. × D. 0.32 cm. (3/8 in. × 7/8 in. × 1/8 in.). Albany Institute of History & Art, x1940.600.1009.20.

Mummified dog. Roman Period, ca. 30 BC–AD 395. Linen, pigment, and organic remains, H. 31.12 cm. × W. 8.26 cm. × D. 10.16 cm. (12 1/4 in. × 3 1/4 in. × 4 in.). El-Deir, Kharga Oasis, Egypt. Albany Institute of History & Art, Purchase, 1958.7.4.

Cosmetic jar. New Kingdom, ca. 1550–1069 BC, or later. Alabaster, H. 5.72 cm. × Dia. 4.76 cm. (2 1/4 in. × 1 7/8 in.). Albany Institute of History & Art, gift of Mrs. John Davis, 1940.28.

Lamp. Roman Period, ca. first–fourth centuries AD. Clay, H. 3.20 cm. × L 6.35 cm. × D. 4.45 cm. (1 1/4 in. × 2 1/2 in. × 1 3/4 in.). Albany Institute of History & Art, Purchase, 1958.7.5.

Bread mold. New Kingdom, ca. 1550–1069 BC. Ceramic, L. 20.32 cm. × Dia. 5.72 cm. (8 in. × 2 1/4 in.). Deir el-Bahri, Egypt. Albany Institute of History & Art, Purchase, 1958.7.1.

Grinding stone. New Kingdom to Third Intermediate Period, 20th–22nd Dynasty, ca. 1186–715 BC. Granite, H. 2.54 cm. × Dia. 2.54 cm. (1 in. × 1 in.). Albany Institute of History & Art, Purchase, 1958.7.8.

Palette. New Kingdom to Third Intermediate Period, 20th–22nd Dynasty, ca. 1186–715 BC. Stone, H. 8.26 cm. × L. 10.16 cm. × D. 1.91 cm. (3 1/4 in. × 4 × 3/4 in.). Lisht, Egypt. Albany Institute of History & Art, Purchase, 1958.7.9.

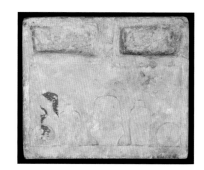

Offering table. Middle Kingdom, ca. 1985–1650 BC. Limestone, H. 20 cm. × L. 24.13 cm. × D. 5.08 cm. (7 7/8 in. × 9 1/2 in. × 2 in.). Lisht, Egypt. Albany Institute of History & Art, gift of Alvord W. Clements, 1964.12.4.

Anubis amulet. Third Intermediate Period, ca. 1069–664 BC. Egyptian faience, H. 7.62 cm. × W. 0.95 cm. × D. 1.91 cm. (3 in. × 3/8 in. × 3/4 in.). Albany Institute of History & Art, Purchase, 1958.7.13.

Ears from a statuette of a cat. Third Intermediate Period, ca. 1069–664 BC. Bronze, H. 8.26 cm. × W. 6.35 cm. × D. 5.08 cm. (3 1/4 in. × 2 1/2 in. × 2 in.). Albany Institute of History & Art, gift of Alvord W. Clements, 1964.12.6a and b.

Shabti in everyday dress. New Kingdom, 19th Dynasty, ca. 1295–1186 BC. Egyptian faience, H. 12.07 cm. × W. 5.40 cm. × D. 2.54 cm. (4 3/4 in. × 2 1/8 in. × 1 in.). Albany Institute of History & Art, gift of Mr. and Mrs. Arnold Cogswell, 1958.32.30.

Sistrum handle with Bes. Third Intermediate Period, ca. 1069–664 BC. Bronze, H. 6.99 cm. × W. 1.91 cm. × D. 0.64 cm (2 3/4 in. × 3/4 in. × 1/4 in.). Albany Institute of History & Art, gift of Alvord W. Clements, 1976.1.1.

Osiris. Late Period to Ptolemaic Period, ca. 664–30 BC. Bronze, H. 19.05 cm. × W. 4.76 cm. × D. 2.54 cm. (7 1/2 in. × 1 7/8 in. × 1 in.). Albany Institute of History & Art, gift of Mr. and Mrs. Arnold Cogswell, 1985.32.31.

Anubis amulet. Late Period, 26th Dynasty, ca. 664–525 BC. Egyptian faience, H. 3.18 cm. × W. 0.95 cm. × D. 1.27 cm. (1 1/4 in. × 3/8 in. × 1/2 in.). Albany Institute of History & Art, gift of Elaine Luizzi, 2005.34.1.

Overseer *shabti* of Ta Wedjet. Third Intermediate Period, 21st Dynasty, ca. 1069–945 BC. Egyptian faience, H. 12.70 cm. × W. 5.08 cm. × D. 4.45 cm. (5 in. × 2 in. × 1 3/4 in.). Thebes, Egypt. Albany Institute of History & Art, gift of Dr. Gerhard L. Weinberg in memory of Max B. and Kate S. Weinberg, 1988.18.

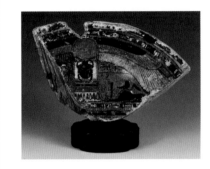

Stela fragment. Third Intermediate Period, 21st Dynasty, ca. 1069–945 BC. Wood and pigment, H. 12.38 cm. × W. 18.42 cm. × D. 1.27 cm. (4 7/8 in. × 7 1/4 in. × 1/2 in.). Albany Institute of History & Art, gift of Dr. Peter Lacovara in honor of Erika Sanger, 2008.15.1.

Shabti. New Kingdom, ca. 1550–1069 BC. Wood and pigment, H. 17.78 cm. × W. 6.99 cm. × D. 3.18 cm. (7 in. × 2 3/4 in. × 1 1/4 in.). Albany Institute of History & Art, gift of Alice M. Schrade in memory of Karl H. Schrade, 2002.15.

Triad of Amun, Mut, and Khons. Third Intermediate Period, ca. 1069–664 BC. Steatite, H. 11.43 cm. × W. 7.62 cm. × D. 3.81 cm. (4 1/2 in. × 3 in. × 1 1/2 in.). Albany Institute of History & Art, gift of Dr. Peter Lacovara in honor of Tammis Groft, 2008.15.2.

Shabti. Third Intermediate Period, 21st Dynasty, ca. 1069–945 BC. Egyptian faience, H. 12.3 cm. × W. 4.7 cm. × D. 2.8 cm. (4 7/8 in. × 1 7/8 in. × 1 1/4 in.). Albany Institute of History & Art, gift of Anthony Lopez, 2009.72.

Osiris statue. Late Period to Ptolemaic Period, ca. 664–30 BC. Bronze, H. 15.24 cm. × W. 5.08 cm. × D. 7.62 cm. (6 in. × 2 in. × 3 in.). Albany Institute of History & Art, gift of Heinrich Medicus, 2013.1.2.

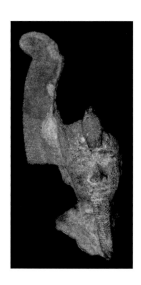

Head of Osiris. Late Period, ca. 664–30 BC. Bronze, H. 11.43 cm. × W. 5.08 cm. × D. 4.45 cm. (4 1/2 in. × 2 in. × 1 3/4 in.). Albany Institute of History & Art, gift of Douglas L. Cohn, DVM in honor of Dr. Peter Lacovara, 2012.38.

Canopic jar lid. New Kingdom, 18th Dynasty, ca. 1550–1295 BC. Ceramic and pigment, H. 8.89 cm. × Dia. 10.80 cm. (3 1/2 in. × 4 1/4 in.). Albany Institute of History & Art, gift of Heinrich Medicus, 2013.1.3.

Tomb relief of offering bearers. New Kingdom, 18th Dynasty, ca. 1550–1295 BC. Limestone, H 16.51 cm. × W 15.88 cm. × D. 3.18 cm. (6 1/2 in. × 6 1/4 in. × 1 1/4 in.). Albany Institute of History & Art, gift of Heinrich Medicus, 2013.1.1.

Shabti of Nefer-ib-re-sa-Neith. Late Period, 26th Dynasty, ca. 664–525 BC. Egyptian faience, H. 19.69 cm. × W. 5.72 cm. × D. 4.76 cm. (7 3/4 in. × 2 1/4 in. × 1 7/8 in.). Albany Institute of History & Art, gift of Heinrich Medicus, 2013.1.4.

Head of a man. New Kingdom, 18th Dynasty, ca. 1550–1295 BC. Granite, H. 15.24 cm. × W. 19.69 cm. × D. 10.80 cm. (6 in. × 7 3/4 in. × 4 1/4 in.). Albany Institute of History & Art, gift of Heinrich Medicus, 2013.1.5.

Tomb statuette. Early Middle Kingdom, 11th Dynasty, ca. 2055–1985 BC. Wood and pigment, H. 19.69 cm. × W. 6.35 cm. × D. 6.35 cm. (7 3/4 in. × 2 1/2 in. × 2 1/2 in.). Albany Institute of History & Art, gift of Heinrich Medicus, 2013.1.8.

Relief fragment. New Kingdom, 18th Dynasty, reign of Akhenaten, ca. 1352–1336 BC. Sandstone, H. 22.86 cm. × 26.04 cm. × 5.08 cm. (9 in. × 10 1/4 in. × 2 in.). Albany Institute of History & Art, gift of Heinrich Medicus, 2013.1.6.

Face of a *shabti* of Seti I. New Kingdom, 19th Dynasty, reign of Seti I, ca. 1294–1279 BC. Egyptian faience, H. 3.81 cm. × W. 3.81 cm. × D. 2.22 cm. (1 1/2 in. × 1 1/2 in. × 7/8 in.). Albany Institute of History & Art, gift of Heinrich Medicus, 2013.1.9.

Statuette of the goddess Mut. Third Intermediate Period, ca. 1069–664 BC. Bronze, H. 17.15 cm. × W. 4.45 cm. × D. 3.81 cm. (6 3/4 in. × 1 3/4 in. × 1 1/2 in.). Albany Institute of History & Art, gift of Heinrich Medicus, 2013.1.7.

Aegis of the goddess Isis. Late Period, ca. 664–332 BC. Bronze, H. 17.15 cm. × W. 11.43 cm. × D. 3.81 cm. (6 3/4 in. × 4 1/2 in. × 1 1/2 in.). Albany Institute of History & Art, gift of Heinrich Medicus, 2013.1.11.

Situla. Late Period to Ptolemaic Period, ca. 664–30 BC. Bronze, H. 17.15 cm. × greatest Dia. 6.35 cm. (6 3/4 in. × 2 1/2 in.). Albany Institute of History & Art, gift of Heinrich Medicus, 2013.1.12.

Shabti of Psamtik. Late Period, 26th Dynasty, ca. 664–525 BC. Egyptian faience, H. 10.16 cm. × W. 2.54 cm. × D. 1.27 cm. (4 in. × 1 in. × 1/2in.). Albany Institute of History & Art, gift of Heinrich Medicus, 2013.1.15.

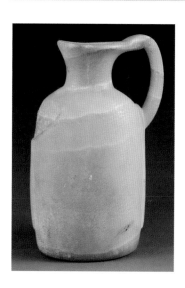

Pitcher. New Kingdom, 18th Dynasty, ca. 1550–1295 BC. Egyptian alabaster (calcite), H. 20.32 cm. × W. 13.97 cm. × Dia. 7.62 cm. (8 in. × 5 1/2 in. × 3 in.). Albany Institute of History & Art, gift of Heinrich Medicus, 2013.1.13.

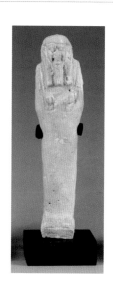

Shabti of Padi-amun. Late Period, 26th Dynasty, ca. 664–525 BC. Egyptian faience, H. 10.80 cm. × W 2.54 cm. × D. 1.27 cm. (4 1/4 in. × 1 in. × 1/2 in.). Albany Institute of History & Art, gift of Heinrich Medicus, 2013.1.17.

Shabti of Psamtik. Late Period, 26th Dynasty, ca. 664–525 BC. Egyptian faience, H. 10.80 cm. × W. 3.18 cm. × D. 1.27 cm. (4 1/4 in. × 1 1/4 in. × 1/2 in.). Albany Institute of History & Art, gift of Heinrich Medicus, 2013.1.14.

Shabti of Padi-amun. Late Period, 26th Dynasty, ca. 664–525 BC. Egyptian faience, H. 12.07 cm. × W. 3.18 cm. × D. 1.91 cm. (4 3/4 in. × 1 1/4 in. × 3/4 in.). Albany Institute of History & Art, gift of Heinrich Medicus, 2013.1.18.

Stela for a sacred ibis. Late to Ptolemaic Period, ca. 664–30 BC. Sandstone, H. 20.32 cm. × W. 13.97 cm. × D. 1.91 cm. (8 in. × 5 1/2 in. × 3/4 in.). Albany Institute of History & Art, gift of Heinrich Medicus, 2013.1.20.

Harpocrates. Late Period to Ptolemaic Period, ca. 664–30 BC. Bronze, H. 9.84 cm. × W. 3.81 cm. × D. 6.35 cm. (3 7/8 in. × 1 1/2 in. × 2 1/2 in.). Albany Institute of History & Art, gift of Heinrich Medicus, 2013.1.24.

Relief of a granary. Middle Kingdom, 11th Dynasty, ca. 2055–1985 BC. Limestone and pigment, H. 16.51 cm. × W. 15.24 cm. × D. 6.99 cm. (6 1/2 in. × 6 in. × 2 3/4 in.). Albany Institute of History & Art, gift of Heinrich Medicus, 2013.1.22.

Votive relief. Ptolemaic Period, ca. 305–30 BC. Limestone, H. 7.62 cm. × W. 9.53 cm. × D. 0.64 cm. (3 in. × 3 3/4 in. × 1/4 in.). Albany Institute of History & Art, gift of Heinrich Medicus, 2013.1.27.

Isis and Horus. Late Period to Ptolemaic Period, ca. 664–30 BC. Bronze, H. 12.07 cm. × W. 3.18 cm. × D. 5.08 cm. (4 3/4 in. × 1 1/4 in. × 2 in.). Albany Institute of History & Art, gift of Heinrich Medicus, 2013.1.23.

Ibis. Late Period to Ptolemaic Period, ca. 664–30 BC. Bronze, stone, and wood, H. 9.53 cm. × W. 11.43 cm. × D. 4.76 cm. (3 3/4 in. × 4 1/2 in. × 1 7/8 in.). Albany Institute of History & Art, gift of Heinrich Medicus, 2013.1.28.

Shabti. New Kingdom, ca. 1550–1069 BC. Wood, H. 16.83 cm. × W. 5.72 cm. × D. 3.18 cm. (6 5/8 in. × 2 1/4 in. × 1 1/4 in.). Albany Institute of History & Art, gift of Heinrich Medicus, 2013.1.29.

Divine votaress. Third Intermediate Period, 25th Dynasty, ca. 710–656 BC. Bronze, H. 6.35 cm. × W. 3.81 cm. × D. 2.22 cm. (2 1/2 in. × 1 1/2 in. × 7/8 in.). Albany Institute of History & Art, gift of Heinrich Medicus, 2013.1.32.

Human-headed scarab. New Kingdom, 18th Dynasty, ca. 1550–1292 BC. Glazed steatite, H. 2.5 cm. × W. 2.2 cm. × D. 1.2 cm. (1 in. × 3/4 in. × 1/2 in.). Albany Institute of History & Art, gift of Heinrich Medicus, 2013.1.30.

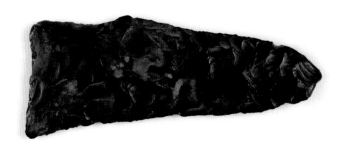

Knife. Late Predynastic–Archaic Period, ca. 3100–2613 BC. Flint, H. 4.45 cm. × L. 20.32 cm. × W. 0.64 cm. (1 3/4 in. × 8 × 1/4 in.). Excavated at Deir el-Bahri, Egypt. Albany Institute of History & Art, gift of Pooh Kaye in memory of Clifford Allen Kaye, 2015.13.

Uraeus with sun disk. Late Period to Ptolemaic Period, ca. 664–30 BC. Bronze, H. 10.16 cm. × W. 3.18 cm. × Dia. 2.54 cm. (4 in. × 1 1/4 in. × 1 in.). Albany Institute of History & Art, gift of Heinrich Medicus, 2013.1.31.

Jar. Predynastic Period, Naqada II, ca. 3500–3200 BC. Nile clay, H. 34.93 cm. × rim dia. 15.24 cm. × greatest dia. 15.88 cm. (13 3/4 in. × 6 in. × 6 1/4 in.). Albany Institute of History & Art, gift of Richard and Joanne Gascoyne, 2015.25.1.

Jar. Predynastic Period, Naqada I, ca. 4000–3500 BC. Nile clay, H. 18.42 cm. × Dia. 12.70 cm. (7 1/4 in. × 5 in.). Albany Institute of History & Art, gift of Richard and Joanne Gascoyne, 2015.25.2.

Face from coffin lid. Late Period, ca. 664–332 BC. Wood and pigment, H. 91.4 cm. × W. 40.6 cm. (36 in. × 16 1/4 in.). Albany Institute of History & Art, gift of Sue McGovern-Huffman and Mark Huffman, 2016.36.

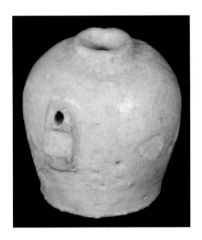

Nemset ritual vase. Late Period, ca. 664–332 BC. Egyptian faience, H. 3.18 cm. × D. 1.91 cm. (1 1/4 in. × 3/4 in.). Albany Institute of History & Art, gift of Julia Schottlander, 2015.47.

Column fragment, accession number 2016. Egypt, New Kingdom, 19th Dynasty, ca. 1295–1187 BC limestone, H. 36.83 cm. × W. 24.13 × D. 39.37 cm. (14 1/2 in. × 9 1/2 in. × 15 1/2 in.). Albany Institute of History & Art, gift of Joop Bollen, 2016.39.

Stela fragment with Mut and Amun. New Kingdom, 18th Dynasty, ca. 1550–1295 BC. Limestone, H. 16.51 cm. × W. 13.97 cm. × D. 3.18 cm. (6 1/2 in. × 5 1/2 in. × 1 1/4 in.). Albany Institute of History & Art, gift in honor of the Albany Institute's 225th birthday, 2016.12.

Sekhmet. Egypt, Late Period, ca. 664–332 BC. Bronze, H. 5.75 cm. × W. 3.17 cm. (2 1/4 in. × 1 1/4 in.). Albany Institute of History & Art, gift of Albert Alston, 2016.45.

EGYPTOMANIA

Egyptian revival scarab bracelet. New Kingdom to Late Period, ca. 1550–664 BC (in probably a French mount, ca. 1870). Gold, Egyptian faience, and glazed steatite, L. 20.32 cm. (8 in.). Albany Institute of History & Art, gift of John Townsend Lansing, 1900.7.1.

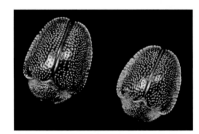

Dried beetles. Late 19th to early 20th century. Organic remains, H. 1.27 cm. × W. 0.95 cm. × D. 0.64 cm. (1/2 in. × 3/8 in. × 1/4 in.). Albany Institute of History & Art, u1991.10 and 11.

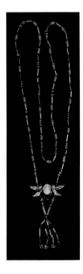

Egyptian revival necklace. New Kingdom to Late Period, ca. 1550–664 BC (with modern additions). Faience, metal, enamel, semi-precious stones, and glass, pendant H. 7.62 cm. × chain L. 76.2 cm. (3 in. × 30 in.). Albany Institute of History & Art, gift of Mrs. Howard S. Paine, u1976.150.

"Best Ginger" spice canister. Bacon, Stickney & Co., ca. 1890. Pine and cardboard, H. 36.20 cm. × D. 30.48 cm. (14 1/4 in. × 12 in.), Circ. 93.98 cm (37 in.). Albany Institute of History & Art, gift of Phoebe Bender, 1991.28.

Secretary. Probably French, ca. 1890–1900. Mahogany, gilded bronze, mirrored glass, and marble, H. 127.64 cm. × W. 81.28 cm. × D. 44.45 cm. (50 1/4 in. × 32 in. × 17 1/2 in.). Albany Institute of History & Art, gift of Stephen Van Rensselaer Crosby, 1957.70.10.

Parlor stove. Ransom & Rathbone, Albany, New York, ca. 1840–1844. Cast iron, H. 123.19 cm. × W. 90.17 cm. × D. 49.53 cm. (48 1/2 in. × 35 1/2 in. × 19 1/2 in.). Albany Institute of History & Art, gift of John Mesick, 2008.4.7.

Bust of Queen Tiy. New Kingdom, mid-18th Dynasty, ca. 1390–1352 BC, or possibly modern forgery. Granite, H. 8.26 cm. × W. 8.26 cm. × D. 5.72 cm. (3 1/4 in. × 3 1/4 in. × 2 1/4 in.). Albany Institute of History & Art, gift of Dr. Heinrich Medicus, 2013.1.10.

Stickpin with sphinx amulet. Middle Kingdom, ca. 2055–1650 BC (in an American, late-19th-century mount). Gold and feldspar, H. 4.45 cm. × W. 1.27 cm. × D. 0.64 cm. (1 3/4 in. × 1/2 in. × 1/4 in.). Albany Institute of History & Art, gift of Dr. Peter Lacovara in memory of Raymond Naggiar, 2015.48.

Relief fragment of a King and god. Middle Kingdom, ca. 2055–1650 BC, or modern forgery. Limestone, H. 22.86 cm. × W. 19.69 cm. × D. 2.54 cm. (9 in. × 7 3/4 in. × 1 in.). Albany Institute of History & Art, gift of Heinrich Medicus, 2013.1.21.

Samuel W. Brown. Unidentified photographer, ca. 1900. Sepia-toned gelatin silver print, H. 25.40 cm. × W. 20.32 cm. (10 in. × 8 in.). Albany Institute of History & Art, Albany Art Union Archive, MG79. B113.F28.

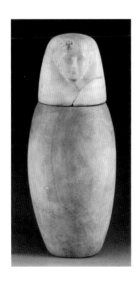

Canopic jar. Late Period, ca. 664–332 BC, or possibly modern forgery. Alabaster, H. 42.55 cm. × Dia. 16.51 cm. (16 3/4 in. × 6 1/2 in.). Albany Institute of History & Art, gift of Heinrich Medicus, 2013.1.25.

View of the New Reservoir of the Albany Water Works Company and the Albany Burgesses Corps. Thayer & Co. Lithographers, ca. 1850. Hand-colored and color-printed lithograph, H. 33.02 cm. × W. 38.42 cm. (13 in. × 15 1/8 in. [sheet]). Ink stamp on right margin: Harriette M. Steele. Albany Institute of History & Art, bequest of Ledyard Cogswell Jr., 1954.59.109.

"The Great Discovery of Mummies at Thebes." August 1881. H. 9.53 cm. × W. 14.61 cm. (3 6/8 in. × 5 6/8 in.). Albany Institute of History & Art, Museum Scrapbook Collection, 9.1.12, page 2.

Letter from Samuel W. Brown to Cuyler Reynolds regarding purchase of mummies. Cairo, Egypt, March 1909. H. 20.96 cm. × W. 27.94 cm. (8 1/4 in. × 11 in.). Albany Institute of History & Art, LIB2007.148_ms-002381.

Letter of John Boyd Thacher to Will H. Low. March 1, 1889. H. 12.70 cm. × W. 21.59 cm. (5 in. × 8 1/2 in.). Albany Institute of History & Art, gift of Alan Goldberg in honor of Phoebe Powell Bender and Matthew Bender, IV, LIB 2003.169.004.

"Seen by an Albanian in Turkey and Egypt: Samuel Brown Brings Back Two Mummies For the Historical Society." May 9, 1909. H. 31.45 cm. × W. 19.69 cm. (12 3/8 in. × 7 6/8 in.). Albany, New York. *The Sunday Press*. Albany Institute of History & Art, Museum Scrapbook Collection, 9.1.12, pg. 131.

Lyon Family in Egypt. Unidentified photographer, 1907. Gelatin silver print, H. 17.15 cm. × W. 22.86 cm. (6 3/4 in. × 9 in.). Inscribed in ink on paper reverse: "1907— Winter, J.B. Lyon Sr. and family." Albany Institute of History & Art, gift of Norman S. Rice, LIB 2010.396.2_PC28.

Postcard of Eden Palace Hotel, Cairo, ca. 1910. Photolithograph on paper, H. 10.16 cm. × W. 15.24 cm. (4 in. × 6 in.). Albany Institute of History & Art, LIB 2011.196.3.

Letter from Samuel W. Brown to A.M. Knapp. March 7, 1916. H. 13.97 cm. × W. 20.32 cm. (5 1/2 in. × 8 in.). Albany, New York. Albany Institute of History & Art, LIB ms-002187.

Egyptian mummies installed at the Albany Institute of History & Art. Photograph by Fellowcrafts Photo Studio, ca. 1926. Photograph, H. 20.32 cm. × W. 25.40 cm. (8 in. × 10 in.). Albany Institute of History & Art, Main Photo Collection, series 52.

Albany Historical and Art Society. Photo by Fellowcrafts Photo Studio, ca. 1926. Gelatin silver print, H. 20.32 cm. × W. 25.40 cm. (8 in. × 10 in.). Albany Institute of History & Art, Main Photo Collection, series 52.

Lyon family in Egypt. Unidentified photographer, 1932. Gelatin silver print, H. 15.88 cm. × W. 21.59 cm. (6 1/4 in. × 8 1/2 in.). Albany Institute of History & Art, gift of Norman S. Rice, LIB 2010.396.2_PC28.

Belzoni, Giovanni, *Narrative of the Operations and Recent Discoveries within the Pyramids, Temples, Tombs, and Excavations in Egypt and Nubia*. London, 1821, 2nd edition, quarto, 533 pp.; one folding map, lithographic frontis, rebacked; plus volume of plates to accompany text, London, 1822, folio, forty-four plates plus six "new plates," hand-colored, quarter leather. Albany Institute of History & Art, gift of Jane Bryant Quinn in honor of David Conrad Quinn, LIB 2005.144.23–24.

Champollion, Jean-Françcois (Le Jeune), *Precis du Systeme Hieroglyphique des Anciens Egyptiens ou Recherches . . . avec un Volume de Planches*. Paris, 1824, octavo, illustrated frontis and sixteen lithographic plates (four folding) in first 410 pp.; plus 45 pp. explanation of plates; plus twenty-one plates; plus eleven more plates, full leather, rebacked, half leather. Albany Institute of History & Art, gift of Jane Bryant Quinn in honor of David Conrad Quinn, LIB 2005.144.22.

Champollion, Jean-François (Le Jeune), *Monuments de L'Egypt et De La Nubie*. Paris, 1835–1847, five volumes (last by E. Prisse d'Avennes), elephant folio, some plates hand-colored, rebound in buckram. Albany Institute of History & Art, gift of Jane Bryant Quinn in honor of David Conrad Quinn, LIB 2005.144.17–21.

Commission des sciences et arts d'Égypte, *Description de l'Égypte: ou, Recueil des observations et des recherches qui ont été faites en Égypte pendant l'expédition de l'Armée française, publié par les ordres de Sa Majesté l'Empereur Napoléon-le-Grande, I planches, A Paris, De L'Imprimerie Imperiale MDCCCIX*. Paris, 1809, partial set, seven folio volumes of text, gold-stamped cloth with leather spines, as follows: Antiquités, Memoires, vols. 1 and 2; Antiquités, Descriptions, vols. 1 and 2; État Moderne, vol. 2, parts 1 and 2; Histoire Naturelle, vol. 2; plus, nine elephant folio volumes. There are seventeen volumes with 681 of the original elephant folio plates, as follows: Antiquities, Descriptions, Planches, vol. 1, 1809, 84 plates (including 1 in color, 4 double page) plus an unnumbered frontis and an extra map bound in; Antiquities, Description, Planches, vol. 2, 1812, 56 plates (including 9 in color); Antiquities, Descriptions, Planches, vol. 3, 1812, 43 plates (including 1 in color); Antiquities, Descriptions, Planches, vol. 4, 1817 rebound, 72 plates (including 4 double, 8 folding); Antiquities, Descriptions, Planches, vol. 5, 1822, 73 plates; Etat Moderne, Planches, vol. 1, 1809, rebound, 83 plates (including 5 double page, 3 double page maps) plus an extra map bound in; Etat Moderne, Planches, vol. 2, 1817, rebound, 87 plates (including 1 double page,1 double page map, 2 folding double plates); Histoire Naturelle, Planches, vol. 2, 1818, 105 plates; vol. part 2, 1809, 77 plates. Description de L'Egypte, preface by M. Fourier, text volume to accompany above. Albany Institute of History & Art, gift of Jane Bryant Quinn in honor of David Conrad Quinn, LIB 2005.144.1-17.

Wilkinson, Sir J. Gardner, *A Second Series of the Manners and Customs of the Ancient Egyptians*. London, 1841, two volume text plus one volume plates (88 plates plus index), octavo, quarter leather with marbled boards, spine labels. Volumes I, II, III, IV, V, and VI. Albany Institute of History & Art, gift of Jane Bryant Quinn in honor of David Conrad Quinn, LIB 2005.144.25-30.

AFRICA

Africa is the world's second-largest and second most-populous continent, after Asia. At about twelve million square miles, it covers 20 percent of the Earth's total land area. Egypt is located in the northeast corner of the African continent.

AMULET

A small token, such as a hieroglyphic symbol or figurine of a god or animal, believed to provide magical protection or other benefits to its wearer.

ANKH

Hieroglyphic symbol meaning "life" and "to live." It was worn by many ancient Egyptians as an amulet, and is frequently depicted in art being held by the gods.

ARTISTIC PERSPECTIVE

Egyptians used variations in size to indicate importance in their art. Viewpoints also changed within images to show the strongest characteristics of objects and people. Faces were shown in profile, eyes were large, and legs were often shown in exaggerated poses.

ATEF

A crown with an ostrich plume on each side and horizontal ram's horns underneath. It is often shown worn by Osiris to symbolize his triumph over death and by the king when performing certain rituals.

BA

The spiritual part of a deceased person that had the ability to act and move about. In ancient Egyptian art, the *ba* of a deceased person appears as a human-headed bird. The *ba* had the power to return to earth and observe the world.

BES

A household god, also associated with drink and revelry. He was depicted as a dwarf with a grimacing, lion-like face.

BOOK OF THE DEAD

Known in ancient Egypt as the book of "Coming Forth by Day." The Book of the Dead is a collection of prayers, magic formulas, and hymns to be used by the soul of the deceased for guidance and protection on its journey to the afterlife. From the New Kingdom to the Roman Period, they were usually written on papyrus and buried with the deceased.

BROAD COLLAR

A piece of jewelry shaped like a bib necklace worn by ancient Egyptians and depicted on images of gods and goddesses. Broad collars were made of natural materials, faience, or gold and semi-precious stones. Because they were sometimes very heavy, counterweights were needed to hang down the back of the wearer to keep them in place.

BRONZE

An alloy of copper and tin, sometimes with the addition of other metals. In ancient Egypt, bronze was commonly used in casting figures of gods. To cast these complex shapes, the ancient Egyptians added lead to the bronze to enable it to be fluid enough to fill intricate molds. The figures to be cast were usually modeled in wax over a clay core; this required less of the expensive metal to produce the sculpture. This technique is referred to as "lost wax casting."

CANOPIC JARS

Containers holding the preserved internal organs of mummified persons. They frequently had lids that were shaped in the form of the Four Sons of Horus: Imsety (human-headed) protected the liver; Hapi (baboon-headed), the lungs; Duamutef (jackal-headed), the stomach; and Qebehsenuef (falcon-headed), the intestines. These four gods were often represented on the coffin as well.

CARTONNAGE

A material made of layers of gummed linen or papyrus and plaster; a medium for mummy masks and coffin decorations.

CARTOUCHE

An oval frame, resembling a tied rope, on which the birth and throne names of the king were written in hieroglyphs.

CERAMICS

Pottery or hollow clay sculpture fired at high temperatures in a kiln or oven to make them harder and stronger.

COFFIN BOARD. *SEE* MUMMY BOARD

CROOK AND FLAIL

From the time of the early Old Kingdom onward throughout the history of ancient Egypt, the crook and flail were part of the king's paraphernalia. Osiris also held them. Originally the crook probably derived from a shepherd's stick. As a hieroglyph, it signified the word "ruler." The flail resembles a fly-whisk.

DEIR EL-BAHRI

A bay in the limestone cliffs in the north part of the Theban necropolis. Deir el-Bahri was used by Mentuhotep II as a backdrop for his mortuary temple during the 11th Dynasty. Later, the 18th Dynasty queen Hatshepsut built her own temple just north of Mentuhotep's that was also terraced and carved into the cliffs. By the 21st Dynasty, it had become an important pilgrimage site.

DEMOTIC

A cursive form of hieroglyphic writing developed in the seventh century BC, written from right to left.

DIVINE VOTARESS

The title of divine votaress, or god's wife, was the highest priestly rank a woman could achieve. During the Nubian 25th Dynasty, the votaresses were sisters of the Nubian king and ruled over Egypt as their representatives.

***DJED*-PILLAR AMULET**

A symbol of stability that was shaped like a spinal column. It was used as an amulet in funerary rituals and placed on the mummy. It also was the sign of Osiris.

EYE OF HORUS. *SEE WEDJET*-EYE

FAIENCE

A self-glazing, nonclay, ceramic material made from crushed quartz and used for large-scale production of jewelry and amulets, *shabti*s, vessels, and architectural decoration. It was often colored blue or green by the addition of copper.

FUNERARY CONE

Cones made from clay set in rows above the entrance of a tomb. Sometimes inscribed with the names of the deceased, their official titles, and the names of their family members, these clay cones have been thought to represent the roofing poles of houses of the living.

GESSO

A mixture of gypsum and glue often used to prepare a surface for painting.

GLASS

A hard material made of silicates and an alkali fused with other substances. It is brittle, transparent, or translucent and considered to be a super-cooled liquid, rather than a true solid. It solidifies from a molten state, in an amorphous rather than a crystalline structure. The earliest known manufactured glass used in Egypt dates from the beginning of the New Kingdom, when it was highly prized and used mostly for jewelry and decorative objects.

HARPOCRATES

The child form of the god Horus.

HETEP DI NESEWT

An offering formula given by a king or god to ensure that an eternal supply of food, drink, and all other necessities of life were provided for the *ka*, the spirit of the deceased that lived on after death.

HIERATIC

The script version of hieroglyphs, it was developed in the Old Kingdom mainly for writing on papyrus; it was written from right to left.

HIEROGLYPH

A Greek word meaning "sacred symbol." In ancient Egypt, one of some 700 signs used in writing. Some symbols indicated sounds, some indicated whole ideas. It could be written from right to left or left to right and is sometimes read backward in religious retrograde texts.

INUNDATION

The annual flooding of the Nile that happened in the summer. The inundation occurred after the appearance of the star Sirius on the horizon and marked the beginning of the new year. In ancient times, this flood washed up over the river's banks and deposited a new layer of fertile soil carried from far upstream.

KA

According to the ancient Egyptians, the part of the soul that was the life force. It was usually represented as a shadow or a person's physical double. The mummy provided a home for the *ka*, and it was essential to keep it (or a semblance of it) intact to ensure the continued existence of the *ka*. The hieroglyph for the *ka* is a pair of upraised arms.

KARNAK

Site of the temple of Amun at Thebes. Called by the Egyptians "Throne of the Two Lands" and "The Finest of Seats," it is one of the largest religious complexes ever constructed. Its 250 acres are the site of temples, chapels, obelisks, statues, orchards, wells, lakes, houses, and storage rooms built over the course of 2,000 years.

LINEN

Fabric made from the spun fibers of the flax plant. It is finer and lighter in weight than wool. Linen was used by the Egyptians for clothing, sheets and bedding, curtains, and sails. The wrappings around mummies were also made from linen—either woven specifically for the funeral or recycled from old household clothing.

LOTUS

An aquatic plant that grew in the Nile. The blue lotus represented rebirth by closing each night and reopening each morning.

MAAT

The concept of balance and rightness in life; a person had the duty to live in accordance with *maat*. The deity by that name (Maat) was charged with establishing and judging truth and honesty.

MENAT

A type of amulet derived from a jewelry element used to counterbalance the broad collars worn by the ancient Egyptians. Eventually, it became more decorative than the necklace it was attached to and was inscribed with spells and prayers. It was a symbol of the goddess Hathor and was often carried by priestesses.

MUMMY BOARD (*ALSO COFFIN BOARD*)

A cover for the mummy in the shape of the lid of the coffin and placed just beneath the lid and on the mummy. Mummy boards began to be made at the end of the New Kingdom and were used only until the end of the 21st Dynasty.

NATRON

A naturally occurring salt used in the mummification process. It is a mixture of sodium chloride (table salt) and sodium bicarbonate (baking soda).

NEFER

The hieroglyphic symbol representing goodness or beauty.

OBSIDIAN KNIFE

A very sharp blade, made from the glassy volcanic rock obsidian, called "Ethiopian stone." It was traditionally used to open the abdominal cavity of a body during mummification.

OFFERING TABLE

The central focus of a cult. In a temple or tomb chapel, there would be a slab for offerings of food and drink. Often these things were depicted on them or written on them in case no offerings were actually brought.

PAPYRUS

A reed that grows along the banks of the Nile River and was used by the ancient Egyptians to make paper. The stems of the plant were pressed together and smoothed to make a sheet, which could be used as a writing surface. In art, images of papyrus plants symbolized the world, which arose from the primeval waters at the time of creation. It was also a symbol of Lower Egypt.

PTAH-SOKAR-OSIRIS

A composite deity combining the creation god Ptah and the funerary deities Sokar and Osiris. Wooden images of the deity were provided in private tombs of the Late Period.

RELIEF

A carved sculpture or section of wall meant to be seen primarily from one direction. In raised relief, the images are raised from a background that has been cut away; in sunk relief, the images themselves are carved into the background.

SARCOPHAGUS

A coffin made of stone.

SCARAB

An amulet used in ancient Egypt, Nubia, and Syria-Palestine taking the form of a stylized scarab beetle. The underside, when flat, could be inscribed and used as a stamp seal. The scarab beetle lays its eggs in a round ball of dung, and the Egyptians equated this with the passage of the sun and with eternal life.

SCAPULAR

A thin strip of red leather with two rectangular tabs at the ends, usually with images of gods. They were worn at the neckline by priests in ancient Egypt and sometimes represented on coffins.

Similar vestments are also worn by Catholic and Anglican priests today.

SHABTI
A small funerary figurine resembling a mummy and holding Osiris's crook and flail. They were developed in the Middle Kingdom and provided in tombs through the Ptolemaic Period. They were usually inscribed with a spell from the Book of the Dead, so the *shabti* could be a servant for the deceased in the afterlife.

SHEN
A hieroglyphic symbol of a coiled rope, meaning "repeat" or "encircle." The *shen* represented the cyclical nature of existence, and when enlarged to contain the name of a king or queen, it became a cartouche.

SISTRUM
A sacred rattle, also associated with the goddesses Bat and Hathor.

SITULA
A ritual vessel for carrying water or other liquids for offerings, usually with a long handle at the top.

SOULS OF PE
Along with the Souls of Nekhen, the mythical ancestors of the ancient Egyptian kings. Pe (Buto) and Nekhen (Hierakonpolis) were early Lower and Upper Egyptian cities and represented two forms of Horus (Horus of Pe and Horus of Nekhen). They were each in turn associated with two of the Four Sons of Horus: Imsety and Hapi with the Souls of Pe, and Qebehsenuef and Duamutef with the Souls of Nekhen. They are also referred to in the Book of the Dead and often depicted on coffins and in tomb decoration.

STELA
Usually a stone slab decorated with relief and/or painted decoration that could serve as a tombstone or historical marker. They could also be made of wood or faience.

TANIS
A city located in the eastern delta of the Nile. The city was sacred to the god Seth, an important trade port, as well as the capital of Egypt in the 21st Dynasty. A large temple was constructed there during this period and was decorated with stone blocks, statues, and obelisks largely taken from other monuments in the area built by Ramesses II, as well as earlier kings of the 12th Dynasty. Now largely destroyed, the temple was considered the northern version of Karnak.

TEMPLE OF MUT
Part of the Karnak temple complex. The Temple of Mut was probably begun by Hatshepsut, although there is evidence that Amenhotep I may have also built a temple on this site. Sacred to the goddess Mut, the wife of Amun of Karnak, the temple precinct was added to with some regularity throughout Egyptian history, growing dramatically under the 25th Dynasty. It reached its present size in the 30th Dynasty. It was even maintained under Roman rule by Emperors Augustus and Tiberius.

THEBES
The Greek name for ancient Waset. Thebes was a district capital that rose to prominence when governors became kings of all Egypt at the end of the 11th Dynasty. It was greatly expanded during the New Kingdom, when Theban pharaohs again ruled Egypt. Western Thebes was a vast cemetery for the residents of the town and for royalty buried in the Valley of the Kings and the Valley of the Queens.

URAEUS
A symbol worn on the front of a royal headdress. The uraeus represents the mythical fire-spitting cobra, a protector of kings and gods, rearing up with its hood outstretched.

WADI
A valley or streambed that is dry, except perhaps in the rainy season.

WEDJET-EYE
The *wedjet* is associated with Horus, the god of the sky, who was depicted as a falcon or as a man with a falcon's head. In a battle with Seth, the god of chaos and confusion, Horus lost his left eye. The wound was healed by the goddess Hathor, and the *wedjet* came to symbolize the process of "making whole" and healing—the word *wedjet* literally meant "sound." The first use of a *wedjet*-eye as an amulet was when Horus used one to bring Osiris back to life. *Wedjet*-eye amulets were placed in mummy wrappings in great numbers because of their regenerative power.

Amenta, A. "The Vatican Coffin Project." In *Thebes in the First Millennium BC*, ed. E. Pischikova, J. Budka, and K. Griffin, 483–99. Newcastle-upon-Tyne, 2014.

Dodson, A. *Afterglow of Empire: Egypt from the Fall of the New Kingdom to the Saite Renaissance*. Cairo, 2012.

Haag, S., and R. Hölzl, eds. *Ein ägyptisches puzzle*. Vienna, 2015.

Ikram, S. *Death and Burial in Ancient Egypt*. Cairo, 2015.

———. *Divine Creatures: Animal Mummies in Ancient Egypt*. Cairo, 2005.

Ikram, S. , and A. Dodson. *The Mummy in Ancient Egypt: Equipping the Dead for Eternity*. London, 1998.

Morkot, R. "Thebes under the Kushites." In *Tombs of the South Asasif Necropolis: Thebes, Karakhamun (TT 223)*, ed. E. Pischikova, 5–22. Cairo, 2014.

Niwiński, A. "The Bab el-Gasus Tomb or the Second Cache of Deir el-Bahari." In *Thebes: City of Gods and Pharaohs*, ed. J. Mynářová and P. Onderka, 176–79. Prague, 2007.

———. "The Bab el-Gusus Tomb and the Royal Cache in Deir el-Bahri." *Journal of Egyptian Archaeology* 70 (1984), 73–81.

———. *Catalogue général des antiquités égyptiennes du Musée du Caire. Nos. 6029–6068: la seconde trouvaille de Deir el-Bahari (sarcophages). Tome 1, fascicule 2*. Cairo, 1995.

Shaw, I., ed. *The Oxford History of Ancient Egypt*. Oxford, 2000.

Reeves, N. *Ancient Egypt: The Great Discoveries, A Year-by-Year Chronicle*. London, 2000.

Singleton, D. "An Investigation of Two Twenty-first Dynasty Painted Coffin Lids (EA 24792 and EA 35287) for Evidence of Materials and Workshop Practices." In *The Theban Necropolis: Past, Present and Future*, ed. N. Strudwick and J. H. Taylor, 83–87. London, 2003.

Sousa, R, ed. *Body, Cosmos and Eternity: New Research Trends in the Iconography and Symbolism of Ancient Egyptian Coffins*. Oxford, 2014.

Strudwick, H., and J. Dawson, eds. *Death on the Nile: Uncovering the Afterlife of Ancient Egypt*. Cambridge, 2016.

Taylor, J. H. *Death and the Afterlife in Ancient Egypt*. London, 2001.

———. *Egyptian Coffins*. Princes Risborough, 1989.

———, ed. *Journey through the Afterlife: Ancient Egyptian Book of the Dead*. London, 2010.

———. *Mummy: the Inside Story*. London, 2004.

———. *Unwrapping a Mummy: the Life, Death and Embalming of Horemkenesi*. London, 1995.

van Rensselaer, M. G. "Ancient Egypt in America." *North American Review*, July 1923, 117–28.

BOB BRIER is an Egyptologist and author affectionately known as "Mr. Mummy." Dr. Brier is recognized as one of the world's foremost experts on mummies and Egyptology. As senior research fellow at Long Island University/LIU Post in Brookville, New York, he has conducted pioneering research in mummification practices and has investigated some of the world's most famous preserved remains, including King Tut, Vladimir Lenin, Ramses the Great, Eva Perón, Marquise Tai (Chinese noblewoman), and the Medici family of Renaissance Italy. He has appeared in many Discovery Channel and Learning Channel documentaries, and he is a featured lecturer on *The Great Courses* (formerly *The Teaching Company*). He has served as director of the National Endowment for the Humanities' "Egyptology Today" program.

SUE H. D'AURIA, who holds B.A. and master's degrees from the University of Pennsylvania, is an Egyptologist who worked for nearly two decades in the Egyptian Department at the Museum of Fine Arts, Boston. She served as an associate curator of the Huntington Museum of Art. D'Auria was a co-curator of the "Mummies and Magic" exhibition at the Museum of Fine Arts, Boston, and served as curator of "Mummy!" at the Huntington Museum of Art.. She has edited several books, including *Scanning the Pharaohs: CT Imaging of the New Kingdom Royal Mummies* and *Ancient Nubia: African Kingdoms on the Nile*.

TAMMIS K. GROFT, executive director of the Albany Institute of History & Art since 2013, has served as chief curator for the museum since 1986. Groft has organized, researched, or supervised the development of over seventy exhibitions reflecting a broad range of topics related to the art, history, and culture of the Upper Hudson Valley and national and international subjects. She has also lectured and published on a variety of topics including nineteenth-century cast-iron stoves, the Hudson River School, American folk art, and nineteenth- and twentieth-century American art, decorative arts, and museum practices. In addition, Groft is an adjunct professor for the Public History Program at the University at Albany and teaches a graduate course called Curatorial Practices. She is currently on the board of directors of the Williamstown

Art Conservation Center, in Williamstown, Massachussetts. Groft received her M.A. in American folk culture in 1979 from the Cooperstown Graduate Program, SUNY Oneonta, and her B.A. in anthropology in 1974 from Hartwick College, Oneonta, New York.

JOYCE HAYNES is a doctoral candidate in Egyptian art and archaeology at the University of Toronto. She has traveled extensively through Egypt and led numerous archaeological tours there. In Nubia she recently completed three seasons of archaeological work at the site of Gebel Barkal. She was site supervisor at excavations in Egypt at Dakhleh Oasis and East Karnak Temple. She worked as a research fellow for Art of the Ancient World at the Museum of Fine Arts, Boston from 1989 to 2009, where she coordinated the Egyptian storage cataloguing project for 70,000 objects at the MFA. At the MFA, she installed the Egyptian Funerary Arts Gallery. She has also been a consultant curator to a number of museums, including the Carlos Museum in Atlanta; Memorial Art Gallery in Rochester; Albany Institute of History & Art; the Museum of Fine Arts in Springfield, Massachussetts; and the Peabody Essex Museum in Salem. She was the co-curator of an Old Kingdom exhibition assembled for the Nagoya Museum in Japan and is coauthor of the accompanying catalog, *Egypt in the Age of the Pharaohs*. She is the author of a number of books on ancient Egypt and Nubia, including *Nubia: Ancient Kingdoms of Africa* and *Egyptian Dynasties*. She is also the author of numerous scholarly articles on ancient Egypt and Nubia.

EMILY JOHNSON CHAPIN earned her associate degree in applied science at Hudson Valley Community College, Troy, New York, in 2008. She is board certified in X-ray, CT scans, and mammography. Chapin has been employed by Albany Medical Center since 2008.

PETER LACOVARA (B.A. 1976, Boston University; Ph.D. 1993 Oriental Institute of the University of Chicago) is director of the Ancient Egyptian Archaeology and Heritage Fund. He was senior curator of ancient Egyptian, Nubian, and Near Eastern art at the Michael C. Carlos Museum from 1998 to 2014. Before that, he served as assistant curator in the department of ancient Egyptian, Nubian, and Near Eastern art at the Museum of Fine Arts, Boston. His archaeological fieldwork has included excavations at the Valley of the Kings at Thebes, Deir el-Ballas, Abydos, Hierakonpolis, and at the Giza Plateau.Currently he is co-directing the excavation of the palace city of Amenhotep III at Malqata in western Thebes with the Metropolitan Museum of Art, and he is working at the site of Deir el-Ballas. His publications include studies on daily life and urbanism in ancient Egypt, Egyptian mortuary traditions, and the material culture of ancient Egypt and Nubia.

HOWARD MAYFORTH is a CT technologist. He earned a degree in radiology technology from Hudson Valley Community College, Troy, New York, in 1997. After working as an X-ray technologist at Columbia Memorial Hospital, he earned his CT Registry from the American Registry of Radiological Technologies in 1999. Mayforth has worked for Albany Medical College as a CT technologist since 2004.

ANDREW OLIVER is a retired art historian and museum administrator living in Washington, DC. After completing his studies at Harvard College, the Warburg Institute in London, and the Institute of Fine Arts at New York University, in 1960 Oliver became assistant curator to the Metropolitan Museum of Art's Greek and Roman department until 1967, and he was associate curator until 1970. He was program associate for the John D. Rockefeller III Fund in 1971–72, a Wilbour fellow of the Brooklyn Museum from 1973 to 1974, and served as director of the Textile Museum from 1975 to 1981. In 1981 he worked as a consultant with The Walters Art Museum in Baltimore and as director of the Museum Program from 1982 to 1984 at the National Endowment for the Arts. Oliver worked as a lecturer and consultant at the Smithsonian Institution, the National Gallery of Art for five years, and as an adjunct professor at Georgetown University's Liberal Studies Program in the fall of 2003 and 2005. He is an author or contributor to numerous books, monographs, articles, and exhibition catalogs in classical and Near Eastern archaeology, art history, and ancient history. Oliver's most recent publication is *American Travelers on the Nile: Early U.S. Visitors to Egypt, 1774–1839*, published by the American University in Cairo Press, 2014.

MICHAEL SCHUSTER is a radiologist. He received his medical degree from University of Iowa College of Medicine in 2009 and completed residencies and fellowships at the Beth Israel Deaconess Medical Center, Boston, from 2001 to 2006. Schuster has worked for Community Care Physicians since 2006 and as assistant program director, Radiology Residency Program, Albany Medical Center, since 2009.

LESLIE RANSICK GAT, principal objects conservator, has worked in private practice and for major museums since 1981. Leslie holds a certificate in art conservation and a master's degree in art history from New York University's Institute of Fine Arts. During her career, she has worked in the objects conservation departments of the Metropolitan Museum of Art, the Brooklyn Museum, and the Museum of Fine Arts, Boston. She is an occasional lecturer at the New York University's Institute of Fine Arts Conservation Center. She is a professional member of the American Institute for the Conservation of Historic and Artistic Works.

ERIN TOOMEY, objects conservator, earned a certificate in art conservation and a master's degree in art history from New York University's Institute of Fine Arts in 2004. Prior to joining the Art Conservation Group, she worked in the objects conservation departments of the Metropolitan Museum of Art and the Brooklyn Museum of Art and as a conservator on an archaeological dig in Greece. Erin is a professional member of the American Institute for the Conservation of Historic and Artistic Works.

PHUONG N. VINH is a diagnostic radiology specialist. Vinh earned his medical degree from the University of Chicago, Pritzker School of Medicine, in 1984; completed a residency in diagnostic radiology from the University of Michigan Hospitals in 1989; and completed a fellowship in neuro and body magnetic resonance imaging at the University of Texas Medical Branch. He has received several awards for his work. He has been associated with Community Care Physicians, Troy, New York, since 1993 and is affiliated with Albany Medical Center, Albany, New York.